W9-BOO-855

DATE DUE

THE TURNING TIDE

MILESTONES IN BLACK AMERICAN HISTORY

THE TURNING TIDE

FROM THE DESEGREGATION OF THE ARMED FORCES TO THE MONTGOMERY BUS BOYCOTT (1948–1956)

Margaret Dornfeld

CHELSEA HOUSE PUBLISHERS
New York   Philadelphia

FRONTISPIECE Pictured in Korea in 1953, a black U.S. marine leads a machine gun squad of Company D, 3rd Battalion, 1st Marines, toward the front lines. By the time of the Korean conflict, the armed forces had become completely desegregated.

ON THE COVER Infantry men of the U.S. Army on the march in Korea during a 1951 offensive.

Chelsea House Publishers
Editorial Director Richard Rennert
Executive Managing Editor Karyn Gullen Browne
Copy Chief Robin James
Picture Editor Adrian G. Allen
Creative Director Robert Mitchell
Art Director Joan Ferrigno
Production Manager Sallye Scott

Milestones in Black American History
Senior Editor Marian W. Taylor
Series Originator and Adviser Benjamin I. Cohen
Series Consultants Clayborne Carson, Darlene Clark Hine

Staff for THE TURNING TIDE
Editorial Assistants Sydra Mallery, Annie McDonnell
Designer Cambraia Magalhães
Picture Researcher Lisa Kirchner

First Printing

1 3 5 7 9 8 6 4 2

Library of Congress Cataloging-in-Publication Data

Dornfeld, Margaret.
    The turning tide, 1948–1956: from the desegregation of the armed forces to the Montgomery bus boycott/Margaret Dornfeld.
        p. cm. — (Milestones in Black American history)
    Includes bibliographical references and index.
        ISBN 0-7910-2256-0.
        ISBN 0-7910-2681-7 (pbk.)
1. Afro-Americans—History—1877–1964. 2. Afro-American—Civil rights. 3. Civil rights movements—United States—History—20th century. 4. United States—Race relations. I. Title. II. Series.
E185.615.D654 1995   94-48331
973'.0496073—dc20   CIP
                                                                          AC

CONTENTS

MILESTONES IN BLACK AMERICAN HISTORY

INTRODUCTION

Black America's historical road reveals milestone after awesome milestone. On the stretch between 1948 and 1956, thousands of young Americans, black and white, went to war in Korea and Vietnam; the National Association for the Advancement of Colored People fought and defeated the restrictive covenants that had long barred blacks from decent housing; diplomat Ralph Bunche became the first African American to win the Nobel Peace Prize, Gwendolyn Brooks the first to receive the Pulitzer Prize for poetry; the U.S. Supreme Court declared segregation in public education illegal. Towering among these historical milestones is one that marks the joining of two roads.

Released from slavery more than eight decades before this era began, African Americans had made costly but steady progress. They had battled poverty, violence, racial hatred. But although blacks' American roots reached deeper than those of many other citizens, some whites still regarded them as not quite *real* Americans. Shockingly, as late as the 1940s, a U.S. senator solemnly asked his peers to approve a bill forcing all black Americans to settle in Africa. The senator met a scornful rebuff, but his words left a shameful echo.

According to law, black Americans and white Americans had equal rights in everything from justice and education to public facilities and housing. But along with *equal* came a mocking qualifier: *separate but*. The legality of the nation's "separate but equal" doctrine had been established in 1896 by the U.S. Supreme Court's notorious *Plessy v. Ferguson* decision. By ruling that blacks could be provided with separate facilities, as long as they were "equal" to those offered whites, the Court had legalized racial segregation. In reality, the facilities available to blacks were rarely equal, but proving inequality, especially to an unsympathetic white society, had always been virtually impossible.

In the years since *Plessy*, the legal swords of such mighty black warriors as Thurgood Marshall, Charles Hamilton Houston, and Walter White had hacked down many of the barriers caging African Americans. By 1948, the segregation of the nation's public schools remained in place (its thrilling defeat would occur in 1954), but countless other roadblocks—the "white primary," racially restricted entry to colleges and graduate schools, black exclusion from juries— had been smashed.

Still standing, however, was one special white fortress: the military. Blacks had served with extraordinary distinction in their nation's conflicts, from the revolution through the first and second world wars. But they had served alone. Right up to the victorious 1945 conclusion of World War II, the American armed forces maintained separate units—as well as separate canteens, barracks, mess halls, and post exchanges—for blacks and whites. A. Philip Randolph and other African American activists had long tilted against the military stone wall, but in vain. Then, in 1948, their efforts finally succeeded, and the wall came tumbling down. Black and white recruits, serving their country with the same valor, now marched on the same road.

THE TURNING TIDE charts the exciting battle in which African Americans finally overcame Jim Crow's military stronghold. And that victory only opens the era's tumultuous story. Subsequent chapters detail the giant strides—and setbacks—that African Americans made on their eventful midcentury journey. Inevitably, their path led to Montgomery, the Alabama city where, in 1956, black America would face one of its toughest—and, ultimately, most satisfying—challenges.

MILESTONES
1948–1956

1948
- February: President Harry S. Truman addresses Congress on civil rights, calling for antilynching laws, anti-poll-tax measures, the creation of a permanent fair employment practices committee, and racial integration in the military.
- March: Truman announces the nation's first peacetime draft; addressing the Senate armed services committee, black labor leader A. Philip Randolph demands desegregation in the armed forces.
- June: Randolph and fellow activist A. J. Muste form the League for Non-Violent Civil Disobedience, a group that advocates draft resistance as a way of fighting military segregation.
- July: Truman issues Executive Order No. 9981, outlawing segregation in the armed forces.
- Birdland, a jazz club named after bebop pioneer Charlie "Bird" Parker, opens in New York City.
- Baseball's Brooklyn Dodgers hire their second black player, Roy Campanella, confirming the team's commitment to integration.
- The Wynonie Harris single "Good Rockin' Tonight" hits number one on the black record charts.
- The Supreme Court rules in *Shelley v. Kraemer* that state courts cannot enforce restrictive covenants that block the sale of homes to black families.

1949
- The U.S. Air Force and Navy move rapidly toward integration; the U.S. Army stalls.
- Trumpeter Miles Davis records pathbreaking "cool" jazz cuts, later to be included in his album *Birth of the Cool*.
- "Trouble Blues," by club singer Charles Brown, reaches number one on the rhythm and blues charts.
- The first black-owned radio station, WERD, opens in Atlanta.
- Jackie Robinson, the first black to play major league baseball, wins the National League's Most Valuable Player award.

1950
- Led by 86-year-old Mary Church Terrell, civil rights activists file suit against Thompson's, a Washington, D.C., cafeteria that violates the city's dormant antidiscrimination codes.

- The United States enters the Korean War; the U.S. Army begins to integrate.
- The U.S. Supreme Court rules in *Sweatt v. Painter* that state graduate and professional schools must admit black students when the state's all-black schools cannot guarantee equal opportunity; in *McLaurin v. Oklahoma*, the Court rules that a black student enrolled at an otherwise all-white school must be treated without racial distinction.
- Chicago poet Gwendolyn Brooks wins the Pulitzer Prize for her second volume of verse, *Annie Allen*.
- Political scientist Ralph Bunche receives the Nobel Peace Prize for his role in resolving the 1948 war in Palestine.

1951

- Sixteen-year-old Barbara Rose Johns leads a student strike to protest inadequate facilities at Robert Moton High School, the only high school blacks can attend in Prince Edward County, Virginia.
- Terrell and others picket whites-only restaurants and lunch counters in Washington, D.C.
- Thousands of whites riot when black war veteran Henry E. Clark, Jr., tries to move into an apartment in Cicero, Illinois, an all-white suburb of Chicago.
- Private William H. Thompson of Brooklyn, New York, receives a posthumous Congressional Medal of Honor for outstanding service in the Korean War.
- Racists bomb the home of Florida National Association for the Advancement of Colored People (NAACP) coordinator H. T. Moore, a major promoter of black voter registration in the South.

1952

- In the Virginia state case *Davis v. County School Board*, NAACP lawyers Oliver Hill and Spottswood Robinson argue on behalf of 117 Robert Moton High School students seeking integration in Prince Edward County schools; they lose the case.
- Ralph Ellison publishes *Invisible Man*.
- Gospel queen Mahalia Jackson conducts her first European tour.
- NAACP counsel Thurgood Marshall and his staff appeal *Davis v. County School Board* and four other state cases against school segregation in the U.S. Supreme Court; the combined appeals become known as *Brown v. Board of Education*.

1953

- James Baldwin publishes *Go Tell It on the Mountain*.
- The U.S. Supreme Court upholds laws guaranteeing blacks admission to restaurants in the District of Columbia.

- Chicago citizens riot over housing rights at the city's Trumbull Park apartment complex.
- The U.S. Supreme Court gives Brown v. Board of Education *a second hearing*.

1954
- The U.S. Army dissolves its last all-black units.
- April: Ruling on *Brown v. Board of Education*, the U.S. Supreme Court declares school segregation unconstitutional.
- September: Schools in Washington, D.C., desegregate; Martin Luther King, Jr., becomes pastor at the Dexter Avenue Baptist Church in Montgomery, Alabama.

1955
- Chuck Berry's "Maybellene" helps usher in the rock and roll era.
- Fourteen-year-old Emmett Till is beaten and killed for approaching a white woman in Money, Mississippi.
- December: Seamstress Rosa Parks is arrested for refusing to give up her seat on a city bus in Montgomery, Alabama.
- Civil rights leaders E. D. Nixon, Ralph Abernathy, Martin Luther King, Jr., and others form the Montgomery Improvement Association (MIA), calling for a boycott of Montgomery buses; the city's black citizens begin walking, bicycling, and sharing rides to work.

1956
- January: In Montgomery, a bomb explodes in the home of Martin Luther King, Jr.
- February: A Montgomery County grand jury indicts more than 100 bus-boycott participants, including King.
- March: Despite the testimony of 28 witnesses protesting discrimination on Montgomery buses, the county court finds King guilty and fines him $500; the boycott continues.
- Rhythm and blues rocker Little Richard records hit singles "Tutti Frutti" and "Long Tall Sally."
- Efforts to integrate public schools spark violence in Mansfield, Texas; Clinton, Tennessee; and Sturgis and Clay, Kentucky.
- November: The U.S. Supreme Court declares Alabama laws requiring segregation on city buses unconstitutional.
- December: Martin Luther King, Jr., and other MIA members integrate buses in Montgomery, Alabama.

1

"DON'T JOIN A JIM CROW ARMY"

In 1945, as World War II came to a close, nearly a million African American men and women returned from military service to civilian life full of pride, hope, and apprehension. The black men and women who served their country during World War II had distinguished themselves on land, in the air, and at sea. Fighting for what President Franklin D. Roosevelt termed the Four Freedoms—freedom of speech, freedom of worship, freedom from want, and freedom from fear—they had enjoyed greater opportunity than any generation before them, and many expected the gains they made during the war years to bring them more power and prosperity when they returned home. But as the decade progressed, most blacks realized that in their own country, the struggle for freedom was just beginning.

For white America, the postwar years were a time of growth and optimism. Between 1945 and 1960, the gross national product (the main measure of the country's economic well-being) climbed 250 percent, and by the mid-1950s, an unprecedented 60 percent of American families had attained a middle-class income. Millions of Americans landed their first white-collar jobs and moved from the cities to the suburbs.

Labor leader A. Philip Randolph (left) heads a line of picketers at the 1948 Democratic National Convention. The protesters were demanding the Democrats' support for ending racial segregation in the U.S. armed forces.

13

By 1959, 75 percent of Americans owned a car and a washing machine, and 87 percent had a television set. After years of austerity—first in the Great Depression and then during the war—most Americans took pleasure in their higher standard of living and looked toward the future with confidence.

The fruits of the postwar economic boom were not divided equally, however. Black families had a share in the nation's new affluence, but racial prejudice often kept them from moving up and even from holding onto the gains they had made during the war. As America demobilized and wartime industries laid off workers, blacks were often the first to go. Black war veterans were officially entitled to the same benefits as their white colleagues, but they sometimes had trouble collecting their due. Lowell Steward, a black pilot who had flown with the renowned 332nd Fighter Group, described the obstacles that faced him in the late 1940s:

> I had a college degree in hand, a teaching credential, went back to get the job promised me when I left for the service, passed a new exam. They wouldn't let me have the job. I got sick of the runaround and decided to become an airline pilot. At the Long Beach Municipal Airport, where they had an army reserve unit flying B-51s, which I was proficient in, they told me they didn't have no niggers at this base. . . . I went to buy a house in Beverly Hills, advertised for sale for veterans. I had the qualifications and the financing. They told me I couldn't buy it.

In many parts of the country, so-called Jim Crow laws—policies that barred blacks from schools, restaurants, theaters, and other public spaces—made it impossible for blacks to live on an equal footing with whites. While most of America prospered, in almost every aspect of life—from housing to education to employment—barriers continued to separate blacks from the privileges enjoyed by white society.

Airman Second Class Philip Wagner checks a sign at Atlanta's railroad station in 1956. Although segregation in the military and in travel between states had ended by this time, the U.S. Supreme Court had not yet outlawed the practice in transportation operating wholly within individual states.

For those blacks who had fought a war against fascism—a racist political system—this failure of American democracy was deeply demoralizing. Indeed, it was a specter that had haunted black troops throughout the war. For nowhere was the gulf that separated black and white America more apparent than in the U.S. armed forces. Blacks had made important strides during World War II, but a basic fact of U.S. military life had continued to remind them that America considered them second-class citizens: U.S. military policy did not allow blacks to live, work, train, or fight side by side with their white comrades-in-arms. Racial segregation remained firmly in place in the armed forces, and most blacks believed that as long as this condition lasted, blacks and whites in the service could never be equal.

It was with energy and conviction, then, that in 1948 black labor leader A. Philip Randolph demanded reform in the U.S. military. That year, as the nation entered the cold war, President Harry S. Truman called for America's first ever peacetime draft bill. If not amended, Randolph realized, Truman's bill

North Carolina men follow local custom by drinking from separate water fountains in 1945. Sixteen years would pass before Americans could visit southern railroad or bus stations without seeing "colored" and "white" signs on public facilities.

could carry the policy of military segregation far into the future. Arguing that "the end of military Jim Crow is the basic key to smashing all discrimination," he set out to convince the U.S. government that only an integrated armed forces could serve as the defender of American ideals.

A preacher's son from Crescent City, Florida, Asa Philip Randolph had entered public life as coeditor of the *Messenger*, a socialist magazine for African Americans. He had formed the first black labor union, the Brotherhood of Sleeping Car Porters, in 1925, and 10 years later he had taken charge of a black political organization known as the National Negro Congress. By 1940, this tall, grave, articulate man had become one of the most active and outspoken leaders in the black community.

Randolph had abandoned religion at an early age, but his Christian background predisposed him to a belief in what he called "the spiritual power of nonviolence." Inspired by the American labor movement and the achievements of the Indian leader Mohandas Gandhi, he became convinced that the way toward racial equality lay in acts of nonviolent protest. Yet unlike the leaders of the largest black political organization of the time, the National Association for the Advancement of Colored People (NAACP), Randolph was a forceful activist, prepared to take serious risks in order to achieve his aims.

During the war, Randolph's militant leadership had helped expand black opportunity both inside and outside the military. By threatening to lead some 100,000 blacks to Washington, D.C., to protest wartime discrimination, in 1941 Randolph persuaded Roosevelt to create the Fair Employment Practices Committee (FEPC), an institution designed to combat racial prejudice in the defense industries. For the next five years, Randolph's so-called March on Washington movement continued to spearhead the fight for equality, as Randolph put it, "in education, in housing, in transportation, and in every other social, economic, and political privilege." The March on Washington movement had been a vital force behind black advancement in the armed forces, yet when it dissolved in 1946, it had failed to achieve one of its primary objectives: the integration of the military.

With the help of Randolph and other civil rights leaders, blacks in the service had won other important gains. Black veterans of World War II had served in more branches of the army than in any previous war, and for the first time, they had also fought in combat units in the navy, the marines, and the air corps. When the Women's Auxiliary Army Corps was established, blacks were admitted, and blacks also gained admission to the women's branch of the navy, the WAVES (Women Accepted for Volunteer Emergency Service). Qualified blacks could attend the same officer candidate schools as whites, and late in 1940, the U.S. War Department opened a training center for black aviation pilots at Tuskegee, Alabama.

Yet as Randolph and other civil rights leaders well knew, such advances could not offset the oppressive message of racial segregation. White military officials argued that the policy helped prevent racial conflict, but to the black men and women it affected, military segregation merely proved that the U.S. government considered blacks inferior. Indeed, the policy brought with it a host of depressing inequities. One black army private who trained at Camp Shenango, Pennsylvania, later described the ordeal to an interviewer:

> The army was an experience unlike anything I've had in my life. I think of two armies, one black, one white. . . . When I arrived [at boot camp], I stepped into mud up to my knees. The troop train was Jim Crow. They had a car for black soldiers and a car for whites. They went to their part and sent us to the ghetto. It seems the army always

arranged to have black soldiers back up against the woods someplace. Isolated. We were never near the main gate. If you went through camp as a visitor, you'd never know black soldiers were there, unless they happened to be working on some menial detail. They didn't have a PX that black soldiers could use. There was a white PX, but we could not use it. . . . They set up a temporary situation in the barracks where a guy had some candy bars and a Coke. At the white PX, you could buy almost anything. We had nothing.

Negro Seabees, members of the all-black division of the U.S. Navy's Construction Battalions, practice landing tactics near Norfolk, Virginia, in 1942. About half of the nation's 1 million black enlisted men served overseas in World War II, but most were confined to segregated service corps.

Conditions like these filled many black soldiers with frustration and bitterness. Military segregation inspired riots at Fort Bragg, Camp Robinson, Camp Davis, Camp Lee, and Fort Dix. At Freeman Field, Indiana, the army arrested more than 100 black officers for trying to enter an officers' club for whites. Although the U.S. War Department made some amendments to the policy as the war progressed—ordering an end to segregation in recreational and transportation facilities in July 1944—its decisions were never strictly enforced, and the basic rule relegating blacks to separate units remained in place until American troops returned home.

After the war, the U.S. armed forces continued to induct blacks according to a quota system. Blacks were allowed to train with white troops in the postwar years, but they rode segregated trains, lived in all-black barracks, shopped at the Negro PX, and watched movies in segregated post theaters. In the late 1940s, segregation was hardly unique to the armed forces. It was practiced in restaurants, schools, buses, and residential neighborhoods throughout the South and in many other parts of the country. But because of the military's direct ties to the federal government, many civil rights advocates saw its segregation as doubly offensive. Randolph, for one, was determined to put a stop to this "government-sponsored program of Jim Crow."

Randolph and his allies took their cue when President Harry Truman gave his first civil rights address

A 2nd Infantry Division squad leader, Sergeant Major Cleveland, uses his machine gun to point out enemy positions to his crew in Korea in 1950. At this point, black and white soldiers had been serving in integrated units for only two years.

to Congress in February 1948. Acting in response to widespread protest over the suppression of black voting rights, in 1946 Truman had created a Committee on Civil Rights to investigate the problems and needs of black America. The committee had come back with bold demands, including antilynching laws, anti-poll-tax measures, and other legislation to protect the rights of black voters, the creation of a permanent fair employment practices committee, and military integration. As Truman spoke out in support of the committee's proposals, black leaders pointed to the military as a chance to turn words into action.

As early as October 1947, Randolph and some 200 black leaders had formed the Committee Against Jim Crow in Military Service and Training, an organization dedicated to military integration. Randolph and Grant Reynolds, a former minister, cochaired the committee, and they began their campaign immediately, calling a conference to rally more prominent blacks to their cause. They turned up the steam in March 1948, when Truman delivered his proposal for universal military training (UMT), the nation's first peacetime draft. Randolph and Reynolds spoke with congressional leaders, mailed a barrage of letters to all the senators and representatives, and finally urged the president himself to make desegregation a part of the UMT program.

On March 31, the two leaders testified before the Senate Armed Services Committee, delivering the U.S. government an ultimatum. Unless the UMT banned segregation and discrimination, they told the committee, they would counsel young men to resist the draft, even in case of

war. "I personally will advise Negroes to refuse
to fight as slaves for a democracy they cannot
possess and cannot enjoy," Randolph informed
the senators. "I personally pledge myself to
openly counsel, aid and abet youth, both white
and Negro, to quarantine any Jim Crow conscrip-
tion system."

Randolph's militancy startled the president, the
Senate committee, and the rest of the defense establishment. In April, a concerned James Forrestal, sec-
retary of defense, invited black leaders to attend a
conference on African Americans in the armed forces.
Neither Randolph nor Reynolds was included in the
National Defense Conference on Negro Affairs, but
those blacks who did participate backed them up by
telling Forrestal and the press that America would
have trouble fighting another war if the military stuck
by the segregation policy.

Yet the military had no desire to take the lead in
the nation's arduous journey toward civil rights. As
much as its leaders were intimidated by black resistance to the draft, they also feared the loss of southern
white support should segregation be abolished. As
August 15—the date Truman proposed to introduce
the new draft—crept nearer, military leaders remained impervious to Randolph's Committee
Against Jim Crow.

On May 7, Randolph and a small party of fellow
activists marched before the White House carrying a
sign that read, "If we must die for our country let us
die as free men—not as Jim Crow slaves," and passing
out buttons that said, "Don't Join a Jim Crow ARMY."
A few days later, Randolph repeated his civil disobedience pledge, calling on the president to abolish
military segregation by executive order.

Proudly bearing his nation's flag, Sergeant Franklin Williams leads his army unit, the 41st Engineers, in a parade-field march at Fort Bragg, North Carolina, in 1942. The majority of World War II's black recruits wound up in such divisions as engineer, transportation, ordinance, or quartermaster.

Despite his bold assertions, Randolph at the time had no way of knowing whether black youth would support a nationwide civil disobedience campaign. Draft resistance meant defying the law, and those who took part in it risked imprisonment. Yet an NAACP poll of black draft-age college students showed that 71 percent backed Randolph's proposal; only 15 percent actively opposed it. Half of those polled said that even in the event of war, they would only serve in an integrated military. Although these figures reflected only the views of the more privileged draft-age blacks, they suggested Randolph was well on his way to a successful movement.

Nineteen forty-eight was an election year, and Randolph picketed both the Democratic and Republican conventions with a sign reading, "Prison Is Better Than Army Jim Crow." A group of draft-age men accompanied him, carrying banners announcing, "We Will Not Register Jim Crow August 15." Apparently sensitive to black public opinion, both parties came out against military segregation in their official platforms. Yet when Congress passed Truman's draft bill that June, it included no provisions for phasing out military Jim Crow.

That same month, Randolph and A. J. Muste, leader of an interracial group known as the Fellowship of Reconciliation (FOR), set to work organizing peaceful resistance to the Jim Crow draft. Their "action committee," known as the League for Non-Violent Civil Disobedience Against Military Segregation, was supposed to encourage youths to resist registration and induction; provide legal aid to those who did resist; and win public support for the campaign by pointing to America's long-standing tradition of civil disobedience. At a protest rally in Harlem, Randolph announced plans for marches in Chicago and New York and a demonstration at the draft registration office in Washington. The league distributed protest buttons and pamphlets containing a "civil disobedience pledge" for draft-age men to sign and return, and a team of attorneys promised to defend those who went through with the league's proposals.

As Randolph's movement picked up speed, it drew criticism from many factions, both white and black. Some critics saw the campaign as a reckless endeavor; others considered it treason. Expressing the general view of the white press, an editor from the *New York World Telegram* argued that Randolph and Reynolds were doing "their race and their country a great disservice." Even most of the black press, though it agreed with Randolph's aims, regarded his actions as overly drastic. Randolph won the guarded sympathy of the nation's largest black political organizations, the NAACP and the National Urban League, but neither association officially endorsed his program of draft resistance. Meanwhile, philosophical differences between the members of FOR and the Committee Against Jim Crow caused discord within the league, weakening its impact.

Yet for all these setbacks, the League for Non-

Violent Civil Disobedience proved a powerful force. In July 1948, Randolph and Reynolds wrote a letter to Truman urging a quick response to the recent "bipartisan mandate to end military segregation." At this point Truman was facing pressure on several fronts. America had recently agreed to host the newly formed United Nations, whose charter promised the support of human rights "without distinction to race, sex, language, or religion." Now that the United States was taking center stage as the standard-bearer of democracy, to Truman and other government leaders, the nation's sketchy civil rights record was becoming a source of embarrassment. Perhaps more to the

Second Lieutenant Mildred L. Osby, a recruiting officer in the Women's Army Auxiliary Corps (WAAC), looks up from her desk in 1942. Like the regular army, the women's service remained segregated throughout World War II; unlike the regular army, however, it allowed black officers to command white enlistees. Of the corps's 6,500 black members, 146 served as officers.

point, in 1948 the president was fighting for reelection. Now that Randolph had called attention to the segregation issue, Truman could not ignore it without losing the black vote—an element of support he desperately needed.

On July 26, after the arrest of more than 30 draft resisters, Truman capitulated. Issuing Executive Order No. 9981, which called for "equality of treatment and opportunity for all persons in the armed services without regard to race, color, religion, or national origin," the president informed Randolph and Reynolds that he was outlawing military segregation. Some three weeks after the order was announced, Randolph and Reynolds brought their nascent civil disobedience campaign to a close. The Committee Against Jim Crow remained intact, however, and pushed for the speedy enactment of Truman's order.

The air force and the navy were the first to embrace the new government policy. Working under the guidance of an interracial committee headed by former U.S. solicitor general Charles H. Fahy, in 1949 the air force submitted a plan for the breakup of its main all-black unit, the 332nd Fighter Group, and for the abolition of its 10-percent quota on enlistments. Within eight months, 75 percent of its black members were serving in integrated units. The navy, meanwhile, had begun the process of desegregation as early as 1946. Its main task now was to attract more blacks and especially to increase its number of black officers. This could only happen slowly, but navy leaders were cooperative, and from 1949 to 1950 the number of black commissioned officers in the branch had grown from 4 to 17.

Captain Benjamin Oliver Davis, Jr., boards an advanced trainer at the school for black air force cadets in Tuskegee, Alabama, in 1942. Like his celebrated father, General Benjamin O. Davis, Sr., the young flying ace would end the war as an American hero.

The army, which had the highest percentage of blacks, proved most resistant. Despite the advice of the Fahy Committee, until 1950 army leaders made no provisions for desegregating their main units, promising only to abandon some of their quotas, improve their promotion system, and increase training opportunities for blacks. Even these promises went largely unfulfilled until the onset of the Korean War in June 1950.

For reasons that were more practical than moral, the U.S. campaign against North Korea hastened army integration dramatically. Although many army officers opposed the spirit of desegregation, as they struggled to organize U.S. troops for this new conflict, they came to believe that an integrated army would simply be more efficient. Brigadier General Frank McConnell, the white commander of a draftee training division at Fort Jackson, told a reporter it was basically too much trouble to segregate recruits. "I tried to sort them by color," he said, "but they began pouring in more rapidly; we got up to 1,000 recruits a day. Arriving without any pattern, busloads of Negroes, then busloads of whites, it was totally impractical to sort them out." McConnell finally took Truman's order at its word and, without formal authorization, began assigning blacks and whites to the same platoons.

Once on the battlefield, the army decided that its all-black units constituted a weak link in U.S. defenses. They also found that when black troops were integrated, their performance swiftly improved. On July 31, 1950, Matthew B. Ridgway, commander of U.N. forces in Korea, began integrating blacks in his combat zone. Seeing that this change went smoothly, other commanders in Korea followed suit, and soon army units at U.S. training posts and at bases in Europe were being desegregated as well. By the end of the Korean War in 1953, the army was virtually integrated. Its last all-black units were broken up within the following year. Much to the surprise of many white officers, the army's white troops took the transition well. Some white commanders even reported that integration made their formerly all-white units tighter and more cohesive than ever before.

The change had been slow in coming, but when it came, Randolph and others in the black community gave it their approval. *Ebony* magazine published several stories on the new military policy in the early 1950s—including one entitled "Every GI a King"—and the NAACP commended the armed services at its 1953 and 1954 conventions. "A lot of us Negroes never had it so good," one black army sergeant told a reporter.

"The young Negro in uniform feels big in it. It shows he's an American and that he's as good as anyone else."

As in World War II, many blacks who took part in the Korean conflict won acclaim for their outstanding service. Pfc. William H. Thompson of Brooklyn, New York, who died at his machine gun during a North Korean attack, received a posthumous Medal of Honor in 1951, the first such award granted to a black soldier since the Spanish-American War. Benjamin O. Davis, Jr., who had commanded the 51st Fighter Interceptor Wing in Korea, became the first black general in the U.S. Air Force shortly after the war. Such honors seemed to confirm the U.S. commitment to the rights of black soldiers; they also suggested that the military was one place where blacks could advance and be recognized for their achievements. Having finally set an example for the rest of the nation, the U.S. military gained a new image in the eyes of black America, and from the mid-1950s on, black support for the U.S. armed forces would remain strong.

Meanwhile, the driving force behind military integration, A. Philip Randolph and the other members of the Committee Against Jim Crow, turned toward other projects. Randolph's favored method of protest—nonviolent civil disobedience—would eventually transform race relations in America. Yet if Randolph supposed the rest of American society would embrace racial integration as swiftly as did the military, he was wrong. Writing for the journal *Commentary* in the late 1940s, James Baldwin anticipated the difficult days ahead: "All over Harlem now there is felt the same bitter expectancy with which, in my childhood, we awaited winter; it is coming and it will be hard; there is nothing anyone can do about it."

2

THE RISE OF
RHYTHM AND BLUES

As successful as Truman had been in reforming the armed forces, when it came to the rest of his civil rights promises, his performance left much to be desired. In his second term, Truman took tentative steps to combat discrimination in housing, employment, and other areas, but Congress resisted these measures, and the president, still wary of southern white Democrats, seemed unwilling to push them through. Despite pressure from black political groups, Truman's call for a permanent FEPC died in the Senate. Congress also defeated another fair employment bill, banning discrimination by organizations involved in interstate commerce. Truman himself may have supported civil rights, but he never gave them top priority, and his failure to do so helped slow black political progress for the next several years.

Left to fight their own battles, blacks worked to create a place for themselves in an America that preferred to ignore them. They faced new challenges, for the war years had brought an important change to black America. During and after World War II, millions of blacks moved from their homes in the rural South to cities all over the nation. In the 1940s, the

The Dixie Hummingbirds assemble for a 1950 publicity shot. One of the first gospel-group successes of the era, the Hummingbirds inspired a flock of imitators, but nobody surpassed them in singing tight harmonies.

31

black population in the Los Angeles area grew by more than half a million; in New York, Chicago, Detroit, and San Francisco, the number of black residents also swelled. For many who took part in this mass migration, city life meant new problems: unemployment, poor housing, crime, drug addiction, and police brutality. Yet the move to the cities also provided the foundation for new and empowering developments in black community life and especially in black culture. Some of the most dramatic advances blacks made during the immediate postwar era occurred not in politics but in music.

By the late 1940s, black musicians had already made a huge impact on American popular culture, leading the nation into the early days of jazz and on through the swing, big band, and bebop eras. Nineteen forty-eight was the year a club named Birdland opened on New York's Upper West Side, honoring Charlie "Bird" Parker, a saxophonist who along with

A southern mother and son make a rest stop on their way north. Between the early 1940s and the mid-1960s, more than 5 million African Americans left the farms of the Deep South and headed for such cities as New York, Chicago, and Detroit.

Black Chicagoans warily stroll the ghetto's mean streets in 1941. Overcrowded and undermaintained, the city's infamous South Side gave transplanted southerners a quick and brutal introduction to life in the "Promised Land," as they had once labeled the North.

trumpeter Dizzy Gillespie had ushered in the bebop sound. The uneven rhythms of bebop had given jazz a new character—no longer suitable for dancing, it now appealed more to the musicians themselves, and to a small following of serious listeners, than it did to the general public. Yet even as Parker, Gillespie, and other pioneering beboppers were changing the course of jazz and attracting a loyal following of white intellectuals in so doing, many black musicians were ready to head in a new direction. In 1950, Parker, a longtime heroin user, lost his professional license on narcotics charges, and he could no longer play in the club that bore his name. That same year Gillespie's group dissolved, and he stepped back from the jazz vanguard, though he continued to play with smaller groups throughout the early 1950s.

Meanwhile, a young trumpeter named Miles Davis was recording the tunes that defined a post-bebop style known as cool jazz. The son of a well-respected dentist, Davis had grown up in a middle-class neighborhood in Saint Louis, where he received training in both the classical and jazz traditions. After graduating from a predominantly white high school, he had gone on to study at the Juilliard School in New York and to frequent the 52nd Street clubs where Charlie Parker played. Davis eventually became part of the bebop circle and appeared on some of Parker's most successful recordings. In 1948 he formed his own nine-piece ensemble, incorporating such unorthodox instruments as the French horn and tuba, and in 1949 he recorded 8 of the 12 cuts that later went into the Capitol album *Birth of the Cool*. Marked by restraint and a smooth serenity, the cool style helped popularize the whole notion of "cool," an attitude of detachment that seemed rooted in black experience. Looking back on this time in his 1963 book *Blues People*, black man of letters LeRoi Jones (now Amiri Baraka) wrote:

> The term *cool* in its original context meant a specific reaction to the world, a specific relationship to one's environment. . . . To be *cool* was, in its most accessible meaning, to be calm, even unimpressed, by what horror the world might daily propose. As a term used by Negroes, the horror, etc., might be simply the deadeningly predictable mind of white America.

As compelling as jazz had become in the hands of a sophisticated trumpeter like Davis, more popular was the new music that took its place in the dance halls. While loyal jazz enthusiasts continued to gather in the clubs to hear the stars of bebop and the cool style, other urban blacks danced to the rhythms of Milt Larkins, Lionel Hampton, and Billy Eckstine and their bands, who toured the country playing for dance crowds in cities large and small. Inspired by the black-led big bands that came out of Kansas City in the 1920s and featuring saxophone and vocals, these combos aimed above all to create energy and excitement on the dance floor. Black Muslim leader Malcolm X, who once worked as a shoeshine boy in Boston's Roseland ballroom, described the mood their music generated:

> The band, the spectators and the dancers, would be making the Roseland feel like a big rocking ship. The spotlight

would be turning, pink, yellow, green, and blue, picking up the couples lindy-hopping as if they had gone mad. "Wail, man, wail!" people would be shouting at the band; and it *would* be wailing, until first one and then another couple just ran out of strength and stumbled off toward the crowd, exhausted and soaked with sweat.

Eventually the big bands diminished in size, and the singers and saxmen took center stage. Vocalists Joe Turner, Eddie Vinson, Wynonie Harris, and Bull-moose Jackson made their mark on the black music scene by putting their personal style into songs with familiar blues melodies and suggestive lyrics. Vinson's "I'm Weak but I'm Willing" and Harris's "Lovin' Machine," to name two examples, contrasted sharply with the sentimentality of white popular songs of the same period.

Birdland (pictured in 1956) exerted a magnetic pull on jazz fans the world over. In its decade or so of glory, the subterranean Broadway club featured every top jazz act in the business, from the "hot" Charlie "Bird" Parker to his protégé, the "cool" Miles Davis.

From the mid-1940s to the early 1950s, Louis Jordan and his Tympany Five rocked the dance halls with a boogie-based style called jump blues, now regarded as one of the major forerunners of rock and roll. In addition to good-natured complaints about women, money, and hard luck, Jordan's lyrics contained subtle commentary on the grim realities of black life in a white-run world. His 1951 hit "Saturday Night Fish Fry," for instance, tells the story of a New Orleans party that ends in a police raid, summed up in the lines, "I didn't know we were breaking the law/ But someone reached up and hit me on the jaw." Variations on Jordan's jump blues were developed by T-Bone Walker, who introduced electric guitar, Chuck Willis, an Atlanta-born singer with a soft, light tone, and Fats Domino, whose expressive vocals gave the music more emotion.

Alto sax genius Charlie Parker, 30, takes a 1950 Birdland bow with master bebopper Dizzy Gillespie. Sidemen for the stellar pair include bassist Tommy Potter and tenor saxophonist John Coltrane.

In the summer of 1949, *Billboard*, the main trade magazine for the popular music recording industry, adopted the term *rhythm and blues* to identify music intended for black listeners. Replacing the outdated expression *race records*, this new designation called attention to the evolution not only of the dance hall bands but of a wide range of other blues- and jazz-based styles. While the jump blues combos were shaking dance floors in black neighborhoods across the nation, a slower, softer, more intimate blues sound was evolving in the nightclubs of Los Angeles and Oakland. In the West Coast clubs, blacks and whites mingled more freely than they did in the East and South, and most black singers there strove to appeal to both audiences. Celebrated crooner Nat "King" Cole adopted a style in keeping with the white popular music of the period rather than embracing the blues, and ultimately he enjoyed a larger listening audience among whites than blacks. Other club singers, including the suave Charles Brown, the versatile Ivory Joe Hunter, and World War II veteran Cecil Gant, billed as the "GI Sing-Sation," brought a light, melancholy blues to both black and white listeners.

Starting around 1950, another blues style, sprung from the raw, emotionally charged musical traditions of the Mississippi Delta, spread north and took hold in Memphis and Chicago. The first artist to make an impression with these "down-home" blues was Muddy Waters, who moved to Chicago in the mid-1940s and became one of the city's best-selling black recording artists in the decade that followed. Waters played electric guitar and shouted rather than sang his lyrics; his rhythms were irregular, his tone aggressive and confident. In 1952, Howlin' Wolf brought his own version of the Delta blues, featuring harmonica, guitar, and harsh, dramatic vocals, to Chicago. Not long afterward B. B. King, Sonny Boy Williamson, Elmore James, and John Lee Hooker arrived to round out what became known as the Chicago sound.

Like the club singers of the West Coast, the Chicago bluesmen made a good part of their living performing in bars and nightclubs. It was by cutting records, however, that they became stars. A few of the most prominent rhythm and blues artists got recorded by such major companies as Columbia, Decca, and Capitol, which began exploring the market for black music after World War II. More important for the better part of black talent, however, were the dozens of small, independent recording companies, known as indies, that emerged in the 1940s and 1950s.

Some of these enterprises were owned and operated by blacks. In 1949 Don Robey, a black nightclub owner and booking agent in Houston, wanted a better recording contract for one of his clients, blues singer Clarence Brown. He solved the problem by opening his own company, Peacock Records, which soon became a major force in the rhythm and blues market. Robey apparently cut a tough figure in black Houston. According to one acquaintance, "He'd have a bunch of heavy guards around him all the time, carrying pistols and that kind of stuff, like a czar of the Negro underworld." Though not always scrupulous about crediting his own musicians—he apparently bought the right to put his own name on a number of rhythm and blues hits—Robey made a great success of his business, recording rhythm and blues and gospel into the 1970s and ending his life, as one associate put it, "a very rich man."

Harlem's Red Robin, another black record company, became an important promoter of doo-wop groups—youthful black ensembles specializing in sweet harmonies and sentimental lyrics. Meanwhile, the majority of black-oriented record companies— such labels as Modern, Aladdin, and Imperial of Los Angeles; Mercury and Chess of Chicago; Duke and Sun of Memphis; and Atlantic of New York—belonged to white businessmen who either admired black music or simply recognized the financial potential that lay in the spirit of rhythm and blues.

Helping the new black-oriented indie labels to prosper were the radio stations that played their records. The year 1949 marked the opening of the first black-owned radio station, Atlanta's WERD. Its original disc jockey, Jack Gibson, remembered later,

> We really didn't know what the hell we were doing, but we were doing it! I would plunk down my nickel every day for the Atlanta *Daily World*, the black newspaper there, and during our newsbreak at noon, I would read all of the stories that pertained to Atlanta. We had no format, so to speak, and we would listen to a white station in Atlanta and copy their format. Whatever they did on Monday, we did, in our own soulful way, on Tuesday, and so on and so on.

Along with white announcers, Gibson's role model was a popular black deejay named Al Benson, also known as the Midnight Gambler, who was one of the first to bring black-style speech to the airwaves. The most successful

rhythm and blues disc jockey of the 1940s, Benson inspired hundreds of deejays, both black and white, to follow his example. One of them, Milwaukee's Eddie O'Jay, later said of him,

Benson killed the King's English and I don't know if he did it on purpose or not. Everybody had to see Al if they wanted to sell to the black market in Chicago, whether it was beer or rugs or Nu Nile hair cream. . . . He wasn't pretending to be white. He sounded black. They knew he was and most of us were proud of the fact. "Here's a black voice coming out of my little radio and we know it's him."

Carrying out their twofold task of promoting records and selling commercial products, the deejays who rode the airwaves in the same style as Benson talked fast, invented rhymes and wordplays, and added appreciative sound effects as they spun their records. Their effusive banter and willingness to offer paying

A star on the rise in 1949, 23-year-old trumpeter Miles Davis warms up for a club session in Manhattan. Davis, who died in 1991, was revered by fellow musicians as the pioneer of cool jazz.

customers extensive airplay could alter the fate of a rhythm and blues single.

As with the rhythm and blues record companies, most black-oriented radio stations were white-owned, and many of them used white deejays who emulated their black colleagues. Although these announcers were usually loyal followers of the black music scene and made a genuine effort to promote black talent, the whole phenomenon of racial role-playing easily went hand in hand with discrimination. A strange twist on the usual story of unfair hiring practices occurred when a black jazz fan named Vernon Winslow applied for an announcing job at his favorite New Orleans station, WJMR. A design instructor at Dillard University, Winslow had fair skin and a northern accent, and it was not until the end of his interview that the station managers realized he was black. When they did, they told him he could never go on the air, then offered him a job teaching their white deejay to speak black dialect. Winslow took the job and made a huge success of his white trainee, to whom he gave the name Poppa Stoppa. After several months choosing records and writing scripts for Poppa, he took the microphone himself one evening and was immediately fired. Fortunately, Winslow went on to better things. Six months after he left WJMR, an advertising agency offered him a job promoting the Jackson Brewing Company on his own radio program. Dubbing himself Dr. Daddy-O, Winslow launched a hit show called "Jivin' with Jax" and soon became black New Orleans's biggest radio sensation, helping to make that city a vital center of rhythm and blues innovation.

By the mid-1950s, both black radio and the rhythm and blues recording industry were flourishing, and it was around this time that another black musical tradition—gospel—entered the mainstream of American popular music. Although the gospel sound had been thriving since the early 1920s, it was not until around 1950 that white America discovered the intense emotion and incredible power that could be generated by a singer like Mahalia Jackson. A longtime favorite in church circles, Jackson had signed a recording contract with Apollo in 1946, and soon afterward her rendition of the W. Herbert Brewster song "Move On Up a Little Higher" became the first gospel record to sell more than a million copies. White jazz critics raved when the Chicago journalist Studs Terkel introduced Jackson on his local television program in 1950, and in 1952 the singer won a prize from the French Academy and made her first European tour. A smashing success abroad, Jackson returned to make another tour of the nation's black churches. In 1954 she appeared on her own radio and TV programs, and soon *Life* magazine was running a story on the acknowledged queen of gospel, showing her cooking soul food for big band leader Duke Ellington.

Mahalia Jackson took the lead, but she was hardly the only musician to ride the gospel train to success in the early 1950s. The Famous Ward Singers, a women's group from Philadelphia, recorded extensively and toured often during this time. Specializing in pop-oriented melodies and eventually exchanging their traditional choir gowns for glamorous dresses, they helped make sparkle and showmanship a central part of the gospel world. Many of the same small record companies that produced rhythm and blues

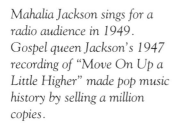

Mahalia Jackson sings for a radio audience in 1949. Gospel queen Jackson's 1947 recording of "Move On Up a Little Higher" made pop music history by selling a million copies.

hits also recorded gospel, and as the sound caught on, some labels made it their focus. Gotham, a Philadelphia company, recorded both the Famous Ward Singers and the Dixie Hummingbirds, a male group whose tight harmonies epitomized small-group gospel. The West Coast label Specialty produced an impressive list of gospel greats, including the Pilgrim Travelers and the Soul Stirrers. Sam Cooke, a lead singer of the last group, went on to become one of the pioneers of soul. Eventually Don Robey of Peacock Records recognized a growing market for gospel. He lured the Dixie Hummingbirds south and also recorded a wide array of other gospel artists, including the Sensational Nightingales and an influential southern group, the Five Blind Boys of Mississippi.

As they gained exposure, these gospel singers, whose vocal flexibility and high emotion created a mood quite different from that of rhythm and blues, began making an impression on the rest of popular music. One of the first rhythm and blues groups to use gospel style, the Dominoes, got together in 1950 under the guidance of a gospel singing instructor named Billy Ward. Although the Dominoes used many of the same vocal techniques as their gospel forerunners, they displayed a sharply different attitude. The good-humored, earthy lyrics of their first release, "Sixty Minute Man," for example, might sound tame in the explicit 1980s and 1990s, but they were nevertheless scarcely suitable for church.

The Dominoes were eventually joined by a profusion of black singing groups that, like the gospel quartets, employed close harmony and simple lyrics to win over their youthful audience. The most successful of these, the Orioles, climbed to the top of the charts after a series of performances in New York nightclubs, where they wore high-fashion suits and helped define the rhythm of their songs with a series of suave, synchronized movements. The Orioles inspired dozens of imitators, many of which—including the Larks, the Robins, the Crows, and the Flamingos—relied on the familiar bird theme for recognition. Specializing in slow, sentimental songs about unfulfilled relationships, these groups were soon outselling the blues singers in the black record market.

Unlike the rhythm and blues hits that went before them, the sweet, romantic songs sung by the groups of the mid-1950s were geared toward teenage listeners, and this was no less true of another musical style that emerged at around the same time: rock and roll. Rooted in jazz, rhythm and blues, gospel, and such white-oriented styles as western swing, Little Richard's "Tutti Frutti," Chuck Berry's "Maybellene," and Bill Haley's "Rock Around the Clock" revolutionized the popular music industry. Often played and sung by blacks but aimed at a young, white audience, rock and roll tapped into a new, large, affluent market and brought enormous wealth to the mainstream recording companies. Unfortunately, it also crushed most of the smaller labels that had made a mission of promoting new black talent, ending the golden era of rhythm and blues.

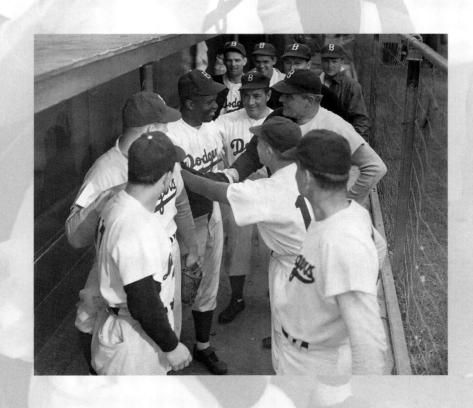

3

THE "NEW NEGRO"

I f music brought strength to the black community
in the postwar years, it also offered relief from the
tensions that came when blacks tried to make their
world expand. For despite the popularity of a select
group of black entertainers, most men and women
who dared to cross the color line in the late 1940s and
early 1950s found loneliness and oppression on the
other side. It was only through long perseverance that
a number of blacks broke new ground during this time,
opening up such fields as sports, politics, business, and
the arts for a new generation.

Perhaps the most celebrated of these trailblazers
was baseball's Jackie Robinson, who in 1947 became
the first black to play in the major leagues. A star
athlete in both high school and college, Robinson was
playing shortstop for a Negro League team, the Kansas
City Monarchs, when the president of the Brooklyn
Dodgers invited him to train for a position in his
organization. After a stellar season with the Montreal
Royals, a minor league team in the Dodgers' farm

*Rookie Jackie Robinson (third from left) beams as his teammates
congratulate him in 1947. The first African American to play in
the major leagues, Robinson faced a torrent of abuse from fans
during his early days with the Brooklyn Dodgers.*

system, Robinson signed up to play second base for Brooklyn, beginning what sportswriters would call "the great experiment." Black fans flocked to Brooklyn's Ebbets Field to see Jackie Robinson smash baseball's color barrier. For his entire first season, spectators read in every run Robinson scored, every base he stole, and every play he executed a sign of what a black man could do in white America.

Robinson got off to a slow start in 1947, but by the summer he was playing brilliantly. To the delight of both black and white Dodgers fans, that season he helped the team win the National League pennant; he also received the Rookie of the Year award from the nation's most widely read sports paper, the *Sporting News*. In 1948 the Dodgers acknowledged Robinson's success by hiring another black player, Roy Campanella, who had developed his talents playing with the all-black Baltimore Elite Giants. Meanwhile, an American League team, the Cleveland Indians, signed up former Negro League players Satchel Paige and Larry Doby.

Baseball seemed willing to give integration a chance, but that hardly meant that the going was easy. From the very beginning, Robinson and the others faced harassment from fans and players who objected to seeing blacks in the major leagues. When the Dodgers and Indians traveled to other cities—especially in the South, but even in such northern cities as Detroit and Philadelphia—they had to deal with discrimination outside the ballpark, as restaurants and hotels refused to give their black players service. Such problems continued even as other major league teams followed the Dodgers' lead and began adding blacks to their rosters.

Roy Campanella (center), the major leagues' second black player, trots across the base after a first-inning home run in 1957. Among those greeting the Dodgers' star catcher is teammate Gil Hodges (number 14).

For Robinson, these racial issues loomed especially large. A passionate man with a history of bitter encounters with prejudice, he refused to let racist comments and actions go by without rebuttal. Once his position in the major leagues was well established, he spoke out on the subject more than the other black players, and his aggressive demeanor made him unpopular with many baseball officials. "As long as I appeared to ignore insult and injury, I was a martyred hero to a lot of people who had sympathy for the underdog," Robinson later wrote. "But the minute I began to sound off—I became a swell-head, wise guy, an 'uppity' nigger." Critics liked to compare Robinson to his teammate Roy Campanella, whose easygoing attitude won the approval of thousands of white fans. Robinson, by contrast, came to symbolize what journalists called the New Negro—outspoken, defiant, and determined to meet racism head-on—a figure even liberal whites sometimes regarded with skepticism.

Whatever controversy his attitude caused, Robinson's athletic powers could not be denied. In 1949, his .342 batting average, his stunning defensive plays, and his outstanding record in stolen bases, hits, runs scored, triples, and runs batted in brought him the National League's Most Valuable Player award. The following year, after receiving a death threat that ordered him not to take part in a doubleheader at Cincinnati's Crosley Field, he answered by hitting a home run in the first game. For the rest of that season and for the following two, Robinson's performance would remain strong. Even as late as 1955, two years before his retirement, his daring baserunning and dynamic action in the field helped push the Dodgers toward their first and only world championship.

Jackie Robinson's athletic feats would ultimately open the doors of the Baseball Hall of Fame to an impressive number of talented black players. While his career was approaching its peak, however, integration progressed slowly. In 1953, only 6 of the 16 major league teams had signed black players. Those blacks who did sign on with the major leagues proved outstanding; from 1947 to 1953, in every season but one, a black player won the Rookie of the Year award, and three blacks besides Robinson were named Most Valuable Player. Although these statistics boded well for the future of black athletics, they also suggested that in order to get a contract with a major league team, a black player had to show not just major league talent, but star potential.

Baseball fans and political groups soon began demanding integration in all of the major league teams, and their campaign was largely successful.

By 1955, only three teams—the Philadelphia Phillies, Detroit Tigers, and Boston Red Sox—still clung to the tenets of Jim Crow, and within the next four years they too would sign black players, confirming once and for all the success of baseball's great experiment.

With good reason, civil rights advocates saw Robinson and his legacy as a major victory for black America. Yet the integration of major league baseball also led to a serious loss: the demise of the Negro Leagues. These organizations, in existence since the 1920s, had made it possible for hundreds of black

Rube Foster, "Father of the Negro Leagues," watches a ball game in the 1940s. First organized in the 1920s, the Negro Leagues made baseball careers possible for hundreds of gifted black players.

San Francisco's Toni Stone, one of the nation's few professional black female ballplayers, exults after signing with the Indianapolis Clowns in 1953. The team hoped Stone's appearance at second base would bolster gate receipts, but by then, the Negro Leagues' slide was irreversible; the Clowns folded in 1955, the rest of the leagues' teams by 1960.

athletes to support themselves playing ball. They also represented one of the few enterprises in which black executives could prosper. Such entrepreneurs as Rube Foster, the founder and president of the first Negro National League, and Robert A. Cole and Horace G. Hall, who owned the Chicago American Giants in the 1930s, not only made the Negro Leagues profitable for extended periods but ensured that their earnings would be funneled back into the black community. As their star players left for the major leagues, however, these organizations—worth $2 million at their peak, near the end of World War II—rapidly declined. By 1953 only four Negro League teams survived. One of them, the Indianapolis Clowns, made baseball history that year by signing a woman to play second base, a young athlete named Toni Stone. The Clowns lasted only another two years after this experiment, and by 1960, the rest of the Negro League teams were gone.

Perhaps more than any other event, the integration of baseball dramatized the problem of race relations for the greater American public. Yet while Robinson, Campanella, Paige, Doby, and such later sports heroes as Willie Mays and Hank Aaron were changing the way Americans viewed their country, blacks were also making strides in quieter ways.

In 1950 the poet Gwendolyn Brooks won the Pulitzer Prize for her second volume of verse, *Annie Allen,* becoming the first African American to win such an award. Based on scenes of ghetto life in her home city, Chicago, Brooks's poems employed language ranging from the erudite to the colloquial. Although she rarely used her poetry as a vehicle of protest, she tried to expose the realities of black life by way of frank, evocative images and a sympathetic tone.

Raised by parents with a strong interest in music and the arts, Brooks began publishing poems at the age of 13, including several in the *Chicago Defender*, the city's leading paper for African American readers. She attended Englewood High School and Wilson Junior College, then combed the streets of Chicago for a job, eventually finding one as an assistant to a phony spiritual adviser. For months Brooks wrote promotional letters from an office on South State Street, a run-down district occupied by derelicts and the poor, only to be fired when she refused to take on the role of "assistant pastor."

After her marriage in 1939, she started attending classes at the Southside Community Art Center, where her writing teacher, Inez Cunningham Stark, encouraged her to develop her poetic talent. Brooks went on to publish works in *Poetry*, a well-regarded literary magazine, and between 1943 and 1945 she won four first prizes in poetry from a series of writers' conferences at Northwestern University. These awards led to the publication of her 1945 collection *A Street in Bronzeville*, which earned widespread acclaim, including a $1,000 award from the American Academy of Arts and Letters and a Guggenheim Fellowship. From that time on Brooks's poems appeared in such prestigious journals as *Harper's*, the *Yale Review*, and a publication for African American authors, *Negro Story*. Three years after her award for *Annie Allen*, she published a novel, *Maud Martha*, which chronicled the coming of age of a young black girl, and in 1956 she produced a children's book, *Bronzeville Boys and Girls*.

While Robinson and Brooks were redefining the boundaries of American sports and literature, blacks were also making an impact on the international scene. The same year Brooks won the Pulitzer, black scholar and statesman Ralph Bunche was awarded one of the world's highest honors for his role in bringing

Born in 1917 in Topeka, Kansas, Gwendolyn Brooks became the first African American to win the Pulitzer Prize for poetry. Along with the prizewinning Annie Allen *(1950), the poet's works include* Maud Martha, A Street in Bronzeville, *and* The Bean Eaters.

the 1948 war in Palestine to a close. Born in a Detroit ghetto and raised in poverty, Bunche had developed a passion for reading at an early age, flourished in high school and college, and ultimately won a scholarship to do graduate work at Harvard University, where he became the first black American to earn a doctorate in political science. During the 1930s, Bunche taught at one of the nation's oldest black colleges, Howard University in Washington, D.C., and conducted research on the social conditions of blacks in America. In 1938 he traveled throughout the South with Swedish sociologist Gunnar Myrdal, carrying out one of the most comprehensive studies of American race relations ever ventured. Myrdal's book *An American Dilemma,* based on their findings, became a classic work in his field.

Bunche's myriad accomplishments soon caught the attention of the U.S. government, and in 1941 the Office of Strategic Services asked him to research the African colonies, where the United States planned to send troops during the war. Bunche took the job and carried it out brilliantly, delivering lengthy reports on the customs, attitudes, economic situations, and political beliefs of African and Near Eastern cultures. Recognizing his contribution, in 1944 the State Department put him in charge of the Division of Territorial Studies, and by the end of the war he was widely known as Washington's resident expert on the colonies.

Bunche had already come a long way from the impoverished world of his childhood, but his intelligence and dedication destined him to go still further. In 1947, at the request of the president, he helped draw up a historic document: the United Nations charter. Soon afterward he was asked to accompany a U.N. commission to the Middle East to help settle the fate of Palestine, where hostilities between Arabs and Jews were escalating. Bunche flew to Tel Aviv and soon found himself shuttling back and forth between Arab and Jewish leaders; gradually he earned the respect of influential people in both camps. When the Jewish National Council proclaimed Israel's existence in the spring of 1948, a full-scale war erupted, and it became Bunche's task to help the official U.N. mediator, a Swedish diplomat named Count Folke Bernadotte, encourage the two sides to come to terms.

Bunche's challenge of a lifetime lay close at hand. After three months of sluggish negotiations, Bernadotte fell to an assassin's bullet, and the United Nations asked the former Howard University professor to take over his role. Back in the United States, Americans were startled to

learn that the new mediator in the Middle East crisis—who up until now had been virtually unknown outside academic and government circles—was a black man. Still, most people were impressed with Bunche's life story, and even the southern press seemed supportive.

As it turned out, Bunche's easy temperament, boundless energy, and thorough grasp of history and culture proved the perfect combination for the task at hand. In January 1949, Bunche manned a council table at the Hôtel des Roses on the Island of Rhodes, coordinating a seemingly endless series of talks between Israeli and Arab leaders. Much to the amazement of those familiar with the long and complex history of enmity dividing Arabs and Jews, after several weeks the delegates reached a truce. As with many armistice treaties, the Rhodes agreement was not to produce a permanent peace in Palestine, but for now, Bunche had won a remarkable victory. The following year, the international community acknowledged his achievement by granting him the Nobel Peace Prize.

Bunche became an American hero after his triumph in the Middle East, feted with parades, banquets, and honorary degrees. His enormous popularity, together with that of such celebrities as Nat "King" Cole, Mahalia Jackson, and Jackie Robinson, proved that by 1950, most Americans were willing to accept and even venerate blacks with exceptional talent. Yet for the majority of African American citizens—working- and middle-class people trying to support a family, maintain a pleasant home, and enjoy a peaceful and productive commu-

nity life—freedom and equality remained a dream.

While such political groups as the NAACP continued to push for social justice in the courts and in Congress, even their smallest advances were often answered with violence. In the late 1940s, for example, civil rights leaders organized a campaign to secure voting rights for blacks in the southern states, and as a result of their efforts, the number of southern black registered voters increased by about a million between 1940 and 1952. Southern racists, however, did not take such developments lying down. On Christmas night, 1951, they bombed the home of Florida NAACP coordinator H. T. Moore, one of the main forces behind black voter registration. Moore was killed and his wife seriously injured in the explosion.

Although the growth of black voting power was mostly a southern fear, just as volatile for northerners

Backed by United Nations security men, Ralph Bunche listens to Arabs and Jews at a 1948 meeting in Palestine. Employing experience, diplomatic skills, and exquisite patience, Bunche managed to bring the two warring factions to a truce—and to earn himself one of the world's highest honors: the Nobel Peace Prize.

Charred debris gives silent witness to the Florida explosion that killed Harry Tyson Moore, state organizer for the National Association for the Advancement of Colored People (NAACP), on Christmas night, 1951. No one was ever arrested for the bombing.

was the issue of segregated housing. Since the early part of the century, when blacks first established communities in the nation's urban centers, white property owners had worked to restrict their freedom. They had adopted real estate deeds that included restrictive covenants—agreements barring the sale of property to nonwhite families. Realtors' associations had discouraged members from showing their black clients homes in white neighborhoods, and banks, fearing the reduction of property values in areas where blacks settled, had refused to give loans to blacks trying to leave the ghetto.

From the 1920s on, NAACP lawyers had fought to get such measures outlawed. Finally, in the 1948 case *Shelley v. Kraemer*, the Supreme Court ruled that state courts could not enforce restrictive covenants, removing at least one barrier to black social mobility. In general, however, white resistance to integrated housing would continue to thrive throughout the 1950s. On July 11, 1951, when black war veteran Henry E. Clark, Jr., tried to move his family into an apartment in Cicero, Illinois, several hundred citizens, accompanied by local police, set fires in the building in an effort to drive Clark away. "Get out of Cicero," the police chief reportedly told Clark during the uproar, "and don't come back to town or you'll get a bullet through you." In 1953 a similar riot flared in the Trumbull Park apartments in Chicago; more than a thousand law enforcement officers were called in to put it down. At about this time, Jackie Robinson was trying to buy a home for his family in suburban New York. The star ballplayer encountered an obstacle at every turn. It was only after two years of evasive treatment from realtors that Robinson met a group of community leaders who were willing to help him, and with their influence, he and his family moved into a house in otherwise all-white Stamford, Connecticut, in 1955.

Robinson, of course, was an exception to the rule. Even when they had legal arguments to back them, most black families lacked the means to take realtors or landlords to court, and this was their only recourse when discrimination blocked their path. Before and after the civil rights legislation of the 1960s, less wealthy blacks would continue to live in Gwendolyn Brooks's "Bronzeville"—all-black neighborhoods where cheaper rents, familiar surroundings, and—all too often—ailing public facilities defined home.

4

"REACHING
FOR THE MOON"

Ralph Ellison, a young black writer, was recovering from an illness at a friend's Vermont home in the summer of 1945 when an idea caught hold of him and would not let him go. So compelling was this inspiration that Ellison abandoned his current project—a novel about a black pilot caught between American and German racism during World War II—and threw his full energy into pursuing the insight he believed he had found. For the next seven years, as he reflected on the significance of his chosen theme, he saw much of his past experience fall into place around it, and ultimately he incorporated his meditations into his first full-length novel. Its opening paragraph contained the words that had haunted him when he began:

> I am an invisible man. . . . I am invisible, understand, simply because people refuse to see me. Like the bodiless heads you see sometimes in circus sideshows, it is as though I have been surrounded by mirrors of hard, distorting glass. When they approach me they see only my surroundings, themselves, or figments of their imagination—indeed, everything and anything except me.

Black children spend a typical school day in Farmville, Virginia, in the 1950s. With no one to help her run the dilapidated one-room facility, the district's lone teacher lets some students play while she instructs others.

Like no novel before it, Ellison's *Invisible Man* captured an elusive truth about the gap between black and white America—one that applied to the New Negro of the postwar years as much as it had to his enslaved grandparents. For Ellison, underlying and transcending the fear, prejudice, and conservatism that impaired American race relations was the failure of whites—and even of blacks—to recognize the African American individual in all his or her complexity.

With its gripping narrative and blunt portrayal of the brutal power relations dividing blacks and whites, Ellison's novel deeply impressed millions of American readers. Published in 1952, it drew praise from critics on its initial release, won the National Book Award for fiction in 1953, and continued to push the problem of race toward the center of public debate for the rest of the decade and on into the civil rights era.

Following close on the heels of Ellison's influential work came another novel destined to open the topic of race relations to a wider American public: James Baldwin's *Go Tell It on the Mountain*. Based on the author's boyhood years in Harlem and the struggles of the generation that preceded him, this 1953 novel offered a vivid portrait of ghetto life, explored the weight of family relations and moral responsibility, and described in intense detail the sometimes confining, sometimes empowering authority of black religious tradition. Baldwin himself, who became a minister in his father's church at the age of 14, left Harlem and his family in order to write this study of black American life: traveling to Paris in 1948, he stayed there for the next 10 years. After the critical and popular success of his first novel, in 1956 he published a collection of essays, *Notes of a Native Son*, which further explored racial issues in the tradition of his early mentor, novelist Richard Wright.

Author James Baldwin strolls through Harlem in the early 1950s. Baldwin's successful first novel, Go Tell It on the Mountain *(1953), presents a gripping picture of growing up black in the inner city.*

Although their final impact cannot be measured, such writers as Brooks, Ellison, and Baldwin, together with their supporters in the white and black press, added fuel to the expanding debate on race relations, and by the mid-1950s, Americans seemed to be examining their society with a new sense of urgency. Still, for some time it was unclear where their reflection would lead. Most whites at this point were willing to concede that blacks had suffered injustices and deserved relief. Yet many also clung to the notion that such relief could be delivered without damage to the Jim Crow legacy. Boldly challenging this claim, black individuals and organizations continued to chip away at the stoutly constructed bulwark of racial segregation.

One successful maneuver in the battle against Jim Crow took place in the nation's capital, where longtime community leader Mary Church Terrell directed a protest action against the city's whites-only eating establishments. A graduate of Oberlin College, Terrell had been fighting for equal rights since the 1890s, when she began lecturing on American race relations in the United States and abroad. Near the turn of the century, when the status of black Americans was approaching an all-time low, Terrell became president of the National Association of Colored Women, a group that sponsored day care and adult education programs in the black neighborhoods of Washington, D.C.

A cofounder of the NAACP, Terrell later participated in the women's suffrage movement, and when the 19th Amendment passed, she became active in the Republican party, urging black women to exercise their new voting rights and throwing her support behind candidates who held out hope for black progress. Terrell contributed articles on black history to such publications as the *Journal of Negro History*, and in 1940 she published an autobiography, *A Colored Woman in a White World*.

By 1949, Terrell had received an honorary doctor of letters degree and gained admittance to the formerly all-white American Association of University Women. She had traveled to London and dined with such luminaries as Emperor Haile Selassie of Ethiopia and Lady Astor, the first woman to serve in the British Parliament. Yet because she was "colored," in Washington, D.C., her home city, there were still theaters, concert halls, restaurants, and drugstore lunch counters that refused her service. Terrell and other civil rights advocates knew that 75 years earlier, the District of Columbia had passed laws against the exclusion of blacks from restaurants, theaters, and public places. These laws had been dropped from statute books in the early 1900s, but they had never been repealed. Realizing they had only to revive the old statutes in order to break down Washington's Jim Crow system, an interracial group of church, social, and labor activists took action. In 1949 they formed the Coordinating Committee for the Enforcement of the District of Columbia Anti-Discrimination Laws. At the age of 86, Mary Church Terrell became its chair.

On January 7, 1950, Terrell and three other committee members entered Thompson's, a cafeteria just two blocks from the White House. The group stood in line, put bowls of soup on their trays, and were ready to sit down with their food when an employee walked up and asked them to leave. That afternoon, the committee filed a complaint with the Corporation Counsel of the District, declaring that Thompson's had violated the city's civil rights laws. The case was to travel slowly from the Washington, D.C., justice system to the U.S. Supreme Court, where it would help decide the fate of a Jim Crow policy more than half a century old.

While they waited for the courts to act, Terrell and others in the committee took their campaign directly to the streets, visiting the owners of dime stores and department stores, trying to persuade them to change their lunch-counter policies voluntarily. After six months, about 20 of these businesses had agreed to open their counters to blacks. Yet hundreds more, following the advice of the Washington Restaurant Association, continued to enforce the Jim Crow rule.

Born in 1863, Mary Church Terrell spent her life battling for social justice. The tireless activist for civil and women's rights was still fighting in the mid-1950s, this time pounding the Washington, D.C., pavement in a crusade to end segregation in the stores and restaurants of the nation's capital.

Undeterred, in the summer of 1951 Terrell and other committee members began distributing leaflets outside the Jim Crow stores, urging customers not to buy their products. They formed picket lines and marched in front of store entrances. Cane in hand, Mary Church Terrell took the lead, and she continued to do so, summer and winter, for the next two years. When she grew tired, she would sit for a while on a folding chair near the sidewalk, but her presence was constant, serving as an inspiration to the others. "When my feet hurt I wasn't going to let a woman 50 years older than I do what I couldn't do," one demonstrator later commented. "I kept on picketing."

Slowly but surely, the committee's persistence bore fruit, as one store owner after another agreed to serve black customers. Then, on June 8, 1953, the U.S. Supreme Court decision came down: the 1872 and 1873 acts guaranteeing blacks admission to restaurants in the District of Columbia remained active and binding. Blacks could eat anywhere, thanks to the committee's action, and anyone who tried to stop them would have to answer to the law. That fall, some 700 people gathered in the ballroom of a leading Washington hotel to help Mary Church Terrell celebrate her 90th birthday. Before she reached 100, her guests assured her, discrimination would be abolished in Washington once and for all.

While Terrell was capping her illustrious career with a successful movement in Washington, some 150 miles away, in Prince Edward County, Virginia, another champion of justice was developing. Bright, lively, and strikingly attractive, Barbara Rose Johns was just 16 years old when she turned one of the South's most oppressive school systems upside down.

Barbara's family owned a tobacco farm five miles south of Farmville, the largest town in Prince Edward County. Like other blacks in the rural South, the Johnses bore more than their share of the region's burdens. Raising tobacco on the thin soil of south central Virginia required long hours of work, but when the family members sold their crop in Farmville, most places where they might relax and enjoy their profits—the town's restaurants, movie theater, and bowling alley—remained out of bounds.

Prince Edward County had always been a stronghold of racial segregation, and most blacks who lived there were resigned to the situation. One exception was Barbara's uncle, Vernon Johns, an ordained Baptist minister whose fiery and articulate sermons challenged blacks in Prince Edward and other Virginia counties to fight for change. Widely read and profoundly disturbed by "the insane hatred between the races," Johns became a role model for his young niece, who worked part-time in his general store.

Barbara attended all-black Robert Moton High School, an apt reminder of the indignities the county's black citizens endured. Built in 1939 on a $40,000 grant from the Public Works Administration and the Virginia State Literary Fund, the one-story school was originally meant to hold no more than 180 students. In 1947, when attendance reached double that number, the county had answered complaints with a stopgap measure—a temporary addition rapidly constructed of wood and tar paper and heated in the winter with stoves.

Unlike Farmville High, the main white school, Moton High had no gymnasium, no lockers, no cafeteria, inadequate toilets, and no auditorium with fixed seats. The buses that took black students to Moton High were mostly secondhand vehicles no longer used by the white schools. The school's science and shop teachers lacked the equipment they needed to teach their courses, and not one of Robert Moton's faculty enjoyed a salary equal to that of Farmville High's teachers.

Fortunately for Moton, the school had forceful allies. Leading the Moton High Parent Teacher Association (PTA) was the Reverend Francis Griffin, the enterprising pastor of the First Baptist Church

M. Boyd Jones, principal of all-black Robert Moton High School in Farmville, Virginia, quietly supported his students' demands for adequate educational facilities. As a result, he lost his job when the students struck to obtain their goals.

in Farmville and president of the local chapter of the NAACP. Supported by John Lancaster, the black county agricultural agent, and M. Boyd Jones, Moton High's ambitious principal, in 1950 Griffin began petitioning the white school board to provide funds for a new black school. For a time it seemed as though the whites might be listening. Most board members agreed that Moton High's facilities were woefully inadequate, and after some negotiation they even appointed a committee to find a site for a new school.

When nothing seemed to come of the board's promises, Griffin and Lancaster offered to do the research themselves. They found an attractive plot south of town for $8,000, but, six months later, the board said that price would have to come down. "We went in time after time, only to come away without anything," Griffin later related. It was becoming all too clear that the school board was in no hurry to spend its money on a school for "colored" students.

By the time she reached her junior year, Barbara Johns had her own ideas about the deplorable state of Moton High. As a member of the school chorus, a drama club, and the student council, she sometimes visited schools outside the county, trips that gave her the chance to see just how Moton compared. Later she recalled:

> The man who drove the bus I took, who was also my history teacher, had to make the fires in the shacks each morning to keep us warm. . . . What really bothered us was the time some of the boys in the vocational program visited the shop at the white school and came back telling us how nice their whole school was—and how well equipped. The comparison made me very angry, and I remember thinking how unfair it was. I kept thinking about it all the way home, I thought about it a lot while I was in bed that night, and I was still thinking about it the next day.

In the fall of 1950, as her view of the situation at Moton gained clarity, Barbara made up her mind to turn her thoughts into action. Meeting with student-body president Carrie Stokes and three other prominent Moton pupils, she spoke of the unequal state of public schools in Prince Edward County, explained what she knew about the PTA's efforts to change things, and asked the other students to join her in an effort to turn the school board's attitude around. Well aware of the inequities they faced at Moton, all four young people agreed. For the next several months, they monitored Griffin's progress with school board officials. When spring came, and he was still getting nowhere, they resolved to take matters into their own hands. Although they were confident that Boyd Jones, Moton's principal, would sympathize with their cause, they also believed he would be obliged to try to

stop them if he knew of their plans, and they continued to work in secret until the time for action came.

On April 23, 1951, shortly before 11:00 A.M., Boyd
Jones answered the telephone in his office at Robert
Moton High. A muffled voice informed him that two
of his students were at the Greyhound station in
Farmville and would be in trouble with the police
unless he came to clear up the situation. Jones left to
investigate, and Barbara Johns moved into the auditorium, where she met briefly with four other students,
supplied them with message slips announcing an as-
sembly, and directed them to deliver the notices to all
the classrooms. By 11:00—the usual time for school
assemblies—some 450 students and about 25 teachers
had gathered in the Moton auditorium.

When the crowd had quieted, the stage curtains
opened, and, backed by her committee, Barbara Johns
announced a strike. Moton High's students had been
treated unfairly for far too long, she explained to her
breathless audience, and it was time things changed.
If the white school board refused to give them the
buildings, buses, and equipment they needed, they
would simply have to refuse to attend school. Those
students who agreed with her aims should walk out of
Moton High that very day, she said, and stay out until
the white authorities responded.

By the time Barbara had finished her speech and
the committee was taking questions from the floor,
Boyd Jones was back at Moton High. The principal
quickly grasped what was happening, rushed into the
auditorium, and begged the students not to proceed
with the strike. Yet he also seemed to respect the
committee's courage and discipline; when Barbara
Johns asked him to leave the auditorium he quietly
complied. Meanwhile, the strike committee issued
their instructions: all students willing to participate
were to stay on campus for the rest of the day. They
could either carry picket signs—which the committee

Spottswood Robinson (left) and Oliver W. Hill report for work in Virginia. The two NAACP lawyers agreed to take on the Moton High case when the students promised to fight for an expanded cause: the end of all school segregation.

members had prepared and stored in the school shop—or simply stay at their desks without opening their books or otherwise taking part in the day's lessons.

That afternoon, the strike committee obtained the name and address of the NAACP special counsel for the southeastern region, then wrote a letter to the counsel's Richmond office asking for legal aid. Later they visited the chairman of the school board and the school superintendent. Both officials told the delegation that their strike was misguided, that their new school would have to wait until its funding had been approved, and that they should return to school immediately; both men also dismissed the student action as a scheme dreamed up by Boyd Jones.

Three days later, a party of Moton students assembled in the basement of Griffin's First Baptist Church to meet NAACP lawyers Oliver Hill and Spottswood Robinson. Both men had been fighting to improve the nation's black schools for more than a decade, and what they knew of Prince Edward County told them that the Moton case was doomed. But when they arrived at the church and saw how far the students had come on their own, they felt obliged to help them see their operation through. Hill and Robinson told the students they would take on their case under one condition: that the students would sue the county school board not for a better school, but for an end to segregation. "It seemed like reaching for the moon," said Barbara Johns some 20 years later. "It was all pretty hard to grasp. But we had great faith in Mr. Robinson and Mr. Hill."

For the next two weeks, while students, parents, and other members of Prince Edward's black community discussed the case with the NAACP lawyers, the Moton strike continued. At the request of Spottswood Robinson, on May 6 the students returned to school. On May 23, Robinson filed a suit at the federal courthouse in Richmond. Named *Davis v. County School Board of Prince Edward County*, the case technically represented the interests of a 14-year-old ninth grader named Dorothy E. Davis and 116 other Moton students who hoped the court would strike down the Virginia state law requiring school segregation.

The last thing the Prince Edward County school board wanted was a struggle over segregation. As soon as the lawsuit had been filed, the board tried to under-cut the NAACP case by securing a $600,000 grant from the state literary fund and forging ahead with the construction of a new school for black students. By the time the case came to trial, in February 1952, the board was able to claim that Moton High's students were demanding changes that school officials had already set in motion. Not only had the county vastly improved black educational facilities over the past 20 years, the board's lawyers argued, but it had recently authorized construction of a new school with facilities so modern it would surpass anything the whites had. Despite testimony from both Boyd Jones, whom the school board had fired some six weeks after the strike began, and Francis Griffin, the NAACP counsel found it hard to convince the court that up until now, the school board had only offered them empty promises.

As for the NAACP argument that segregated schools were inherently unequal, the board's lawyers had at the ready a panel of experts who could prove this was not so. The lawyers knew from other anti-segregation cases that Robinson and Hill would bring scholarly witnesses to the stand, each citing studies showing that segregation damaged both the psyche of black children and their ability to learn. Drawing on research of their own, the witnesses for the defense sought to discredit such studies.

In the end, however, more convincing than any of these arguments was the white lawyers' contention that racial segregation, based on long tradition, was an institution Virginia's whites were not prepared to abandon. Five days after the trial began, the court concluded that segregation caused "no hurt or harm to either race," and that the Prince Edward school board should continue to work toward making its black and white schools equal.

Ready to commence their historic 1952 antisegregation lawsuit, parents and students from Virginia's Robert Moton High School assemble on the steps of the state capitol in Richmond.

Although the NAACP lawyers took the verdict in stride, for the strike committee at Moton, the court's decision came as a heavy blow. Barbara Rose Johns, for her part, received the news calmly in Montgomery, Alabama, where for her own safety she had gone to complete her schooling shortly after the suit was filed. Barbara spent the next few years with her uncle Vernon, who at the time was serving as pastor for Montgomery's Dexter Avenue Baptist Church. In 1954, when Vernon Johns returned to Prince Edward to raise livestock, he was replaced at Dexter by a 27-year-old seminary graduate whose principles closely matched his own. This bold young newcomer, the son of an Atlanta preacher, was the Reverend Martin Luther King, Jr.

5

"MOVE ON UP
A LITTLE HIGHER"

For the black citizens of Prince Edward County, the Moton High case was a momentous event; for the NAACP Legal Defense and Education Fund, it was a step toward an even larger goal. Spottswood Robinson and Oliver Hill may have sympathized with the students at Moton, but for them, the main purpose of *Davis v. County School Board* was to prepare for an attack against segregation at the federal level. The lawyers were following a plan. Before they had ever heard of Robert Moton High School, Thurgood Marshall, chief counsel for the NAACP, had launched a campaign to convince the U.S. Supreme Court that school segregation violated the U.S. Constitution.

When Marshall presented his strategy, NAACP lawyers had already been fighting for improvements in black education for more than 20 years. During the early phase of their campaign, they had decided they stood little chance of winning an all-out battle against school segregation. Instead they had tried to make progress within the Jim Crow system, pushing school districts one by one to improve the condition of their

NAACP chief counsel Thurgood Marshall (second from right) meets with his staff to plan strategy in the upcoming U.S. Supreme Court battle to end school segregation. The case, Brown v. Board of Education of Topeka, would turn out to be a major milestone in American social history.

75

black schools and to raise black teachers' salaries to a level equal with that of whites.

> **The NAACP had helped black education significantly during these years, but by the mid-1940s, its leaders were growing impatient with the laborious task of "equalizing" Jim Crow schools. White school administrators were already finding ways to skirt the equal-pay requirement, citing low performance ratings—based on observation by white officials—as the reason behind black teachers' lower salaries. NAACP lawyers also knew that in the end, the segregation policy was founded on false and bigoted notions: that blacks were intellectually inferior to whites; that black males posed a sexual threat to young white women; that any kind of social contact between black and white children was unhealthy. With ideas like these influencing the minds of both black and white school children, no amount of improvement could make a segregated school system truly equal.**

Believing that the time had come to challenge this centerpiece of Jim Crow tradition, in 1950 chief counsel Marshall told NAACP lawyers to end their school equalization drive and to file suits only on the grounds that segregation itself was illegal. If these cases were defeated in the lower courts, Marshall promised, he would ask the Supreme Court to hear their appeals.

Ultimately, Marshall would have to persuade the Supreme Court to override the verdict of an 1896 case called *Plessy v. Ferguson*. The case concerned a black man named Homer Adolph Plessy, who was convicted for refusing to sit in the "colored" section of a train in Louisiana, where state law required segregation in public facilities. Plessy's lawyer had appealed to the Supreme Court, arguing that the law violated the Fourteenth Amendment, guaranteeing all citizens "the equal protection of the laws." The Court had ruled against him. As long as facilities for blacks and whites remained equal, the Court had decided, the fact that they were separate was immaterial.

Ever since the *Plessy* ruling, the "separate but equal" doctrine had provided backing for thousands of discriminatory state laws. In 1950, 17 states, in addition to the District of Columbia, required segregation in public schools. Four more, although they had no laws against integrated schools, gave local school systems the option of enforcing the Jim Crow rule.

Marshall knew it would be no simple matter to persuade the Supreme Court to overturn *Plessy*, but something in the nation's shifting attitude toward race relations convinced him it was time to try. One cause for optimism was the recent success of A. Philip Randolph's campaign to end military segregation. Another was the victory Marshall himself enjoyed in two 1950 Supreme Court cases challenging segregation in higher education.

In *Sweatt v. Painter*, Marshall appealed the case of a black postal worker named Heman Marion Sweatt, who had applied to the University of Texas Law School and been rejected solely on the basis of his color. When ordered by a Texas judge either to admit Sweatt or open a new, "equal" law school for blacks, Texas had set up a makeshift school consisting of three rented rooms and three part-time instructors. Sweatt had sued again, this time with the aid of Thurgood Marshall, who eventually moved the case from Texas to the U.S. Supreme Court.

There Marshall racked up a subtle but powerful strike against *Plessy*: the Court declared Texas's black law school unequal not only because of its inferior

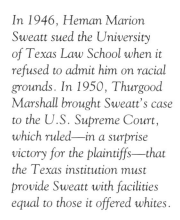

In 1946, Heman Marion Sweatt sued the University of Texas Law School when it refused to admit him on racial grounds. In 1950, Thurgood Marshall brought Sweatt's case to the U.S. Supreme Court, which ruled—in a surprise victory for the plaintiffs—that the Texas institution must provide Sweatt with facilities equal to those it offered whites.

facilities, but because of "qualities which are incapable of objective measurement but which make for the greatness in a law school." If the Court was willing to acknowledge that equality went beyond physical resources, it might also come around to admitting that the whole idea of "separate but equal" was wrong.

The same day the Court heard *Sweatt v. Painter*, it also heard another case against a segregated university, *McLaurin v. Oklahoma State Regents for Higher Education*. In 1948 Marshall had helped a black college instructor, George W. McLaurin, win a suit against the University of Oklahoma. The school had barred McLaurin from a Ph.D. program in education, a program that no black school in the state offered.

Exiled to a lonely desk at the back of a classroom, 54-year-old college instructor George W. McLaurin attends a class in educational sociology at the University of Oklahoma in 1948. McLaurin, the first African American ever enrolled at the university, was also assigned segregated seating in the college library and dining hall.

When the Oklahoma district court ordered the school to admit McLaurin, the school devised a system so that the black doctoral student could remain segregated inside the school. When McLaurin attended lectures, he had to take a seat outside classroom doors; he was seated at a special, screened-off desk when he used the library, and he could eat in the school cafeteria only when no white students were present.

Appalled by this "separate but equal" arrangement, Marshall returned to the district court and argued that the setup at Oklahoma created tensions that were bound to interfere with McLaurin's academic progress. The district court ruled against him, but when he appealed, the Supreme Court took the case, ultimately agreeing that a black student, once admitted to a white school, could not be subjected to further segregation. "Such restrictions," said the Court, "impair and inhibit [the student's] ability to study, engage in discussions, and exchange views with other students, and, in general, to learn his profession."

Buoyed by the results of *Sweatt* and *McLaurin*, Marshall urged NAACP attorneys to aid him in the next step, combating segregation in public schools. Between 1950 and 1952, the lawyers for the Legal Defense and Education Fund brought strong suits against school segregation not only in Prince Edward County, Virginia, but in Delaware, South Carolina, Kansas, and Washington, D.C. Local courts ruled against the plaintiffs in all five cases, and one by one, the Legal Defense and Education Fund submitted them to the Supreme Court for appeal. After some deliberation, the Court decided to consolidate the five cases and give them a single hearing on December 9, 1952. The by-now mammoth NAACP case against school segregation bore the title *Brown v. Board of Education of Topeka*, after the Kansas suit, brought by a Topeka parent named Oliver Brown against the city school board.

Brimming with enthusiasm and anxiety, Marshall and his staff threw themselves into the task of preparing their arguments for the December case. They spent long hours poring over the history of the Fourteenth Amendment, they reviewed study after study dealing with the effects of segregation on childhood education and development, and, with great care, they drafted and continued to refine the briefs they would submit to the Court before the hearing.

Marshall also brought in help from the outside. One ally the NAACP team hoped would prove useful was a 37-year-old sociologist named Kenneth Clark, who had testified in *Davis* as well as two of the other

Linda Brown, the Kansas girl whose name became a synonym for integration (Brown v. Board), stands alone in the yard of a Topeka school. It was Linda's lawsuit (brought by her father) that started the ball rolling toward the 1954 Supreme Court decision that demolished the legal basis for segregation in U.S. public schools.

state cases. Clark had caused controversy in the lower courts by referring to a study he had conducted to measure the influence of segregation on the self-image of young black children. In this experiment, Clark had asked hundreds of black children attending segregated schools to make judgments about four dolls that were identical except for their color: two of the dolls were white and two were brown. When asked which doll they liked best and which looked "bad," Clark reported, the majority of the black children showed "an unmistakable preference for the white doll and a rejection of the brown doll."

The NAACP's opponents in court had sought to discredit the so-called doll test, which, they argued, gave no evidence of a direct connection between segregation and the children's beliefs about race. Although some NAACP lawyers preferred not to rely on sociological arguments of this kind, they were generally pleased with the brief Clark composed for the Supreme Court hearing. Signed by 35 prominent social scientists, Clark's report did not dwell on experimental evidence but argued persuasively that segregation damaged not only the self-esteem of black children but also the moral character of whites. Forcing black and white children to attend separate schools, Clark asserted, obstructed communication between the races and encouraged an attitude of hostility and mistrust. Having studied desegregation efforts in housing developments, in the military, and in industry, Clark concluded that school integration could be accomplished with little conflict, and he urged the Court to endorse it with all its power.

The December hearing lasted three days. Marshall, Robinson, and five other NAACP attorneys argued their case with conviction. Their opponent in court, the eminent southern lawyer John W. Davis, taxed them thoroughly. On December 12, the justices withdrew to discuss the case. Their response did not come until June 1953, when they announced that several points in the case required clarification, which NAACP lawyers could offer at a rehearing on December 7, 1953.

That summer the Legal Defense and Education Fund renewed its grueling routine, researching constitutional history, soliciting advice and information from scholars, and pondering the Court's subtly formulated questions. In late September, Marshall organized a three-day conference during which nearly 100 scholars held seminars to discuss the ins and outs of the Court's request. By the time the second round of briefs was due, the NAACP Legal Defense and Education Fund had enlisted the support of more than 200 historians, legal theorists, political scientists, and educational authorities. Their contributions would prove decisive on the day of the hearing.

Before dawn on December 7, dozens of citizens, both black and white, hoping to observe the final stages of a struggle begun even before Thurgood Marshall's time, lined up outside the U.S. Supreme Court Building. That day and the next, Marshall and his staff hammered home their final arguments, maintaining that *Plessy* could not stand up against the changes America had undergone since the decision was handed down. In his concluding rebuttal, Marshall told the Court:

> I got the feeling on hearing the discussion yesterday that when you put a white child in a school with a whole lot of colored children, the child would fall apart or something. Everybody knows that is not true. Those same kids in Virginia and South Carolina—and I have seen them do it—they play in the streets together, they play on their farms together, they go down the road together, they separate to go to school, they come out of school and play ball together. . . . The only thing [segregation] can be is an inherent determination that the people who were formerly

Fifteen-year-old Spottswood Bolling shares a big smile with his mother, Sarah, as they read of the Supreme Court's historic antisegregation decision in a Washington, D.C., newspaper. Like Linda Brown, Spottswood was a plaintiff in his district's case against the school system.

Residents of Milford, Delaware, sign up for membership in the National Association for the Advancement of White People, a group created in 1954 by Bryant W. Bowles (in suit, next to police officer) to fight integration in the state's schools. Delaware's racists were not alone: similar groups, including White Citizens' Councils, sprang up across the South after the Brown decision.

in slavery, regardless of anything else, shall be kept as near that stage as is possible. And now is the time, we submit, that this Court should make it clear that that is not what our Constitution stands for.

Four months later, Chief Justice Earl Warren read the Supreme Court's decision before a rapt audience. After a meandering introduction discussing the evidence presented by the NAACP staff, the ramifications of the Fourteenth Amendment, the impact of *Plessy v. Ferguson*, and the recent history of black education, including the Supreme Court cases *Sweatt* and *McLaurin*, Warren presented the Court's unanimous verdict:

Does segregation of children in public schools solely on the basis of race, even though the physical facilities and

> other "tangible" factors may be equal, deprive the children of the minority group of equal education opportunities? We believe that it does. . . . We conclude that in the field of public education the doctrine of "separate but equal" has no place.

Civil rights advocates across the nation rejoiced at this triumph for black America, but school segregation did not end with the Court's decree. School officials in Washington, D.C., responded quickly to the ruling, beginning a widespread desegregation effort as early as September 1954. In the southern states, however, the transition would not be so smooth. Most communities in the South elected to take their time in fulfilling the 1954 order, and some vowed to resist it by any means.

In May 1955, the Supreme Court issued a second ruling, now known as *Brown II*, which aimed to guide the nation in carrying out the original antisegregation order. Announcing that America's schools were to act on the *Brown* decision "with all deliberate speed," the Court seemed, to many observers, to be giving southerners license to put off the task indefinitely.

Black leaders did not stand by idly while southern communities ignored the call to integrate. In 1955 the NAACP filed desegregation petitions with 170 school boards in 17 states. That same year, in Mississippi, Alabama, and South Carolina, white supremacist groups known as Citizens' Councils saw to it that blacks who had signed such petitions were fired from their jobs and denied credit by stores and banks in their community. In 1956, efforts to integrate public schools would spark violence in Mansfield, Texas; Clinton, Tennessee; and Sturgis and Clay, Kentucky. Clearly, conservative white southerners recognized *Brown v. Board of Education* for what it was: the critical step in a movement to stamp out racial segregation in every facet of American society, once and for all.

6

MONTGOMERY

Montgomery, Alabama, was not unlike many other small southern cities during the 1950s. For more than half a century, the concept of "separate but equal" had governed relations between whites and blacks, and as far as most whites were concerned, that was as it should be. In Montgomery, custom—and the law—mandated separate facilities for the races, from drinking fountains and restrooms to seats in movie theaters and restaurants to waiting lines in city offices and dressing rooms in department stores.

> The oppression and inequity of Montgomery's segregation policy was especially visible in public transportation. The bulk of the city's African American population used municipal buses to get to and from work. City laws mandated that seating at the front of the buses be reserved for white passengers. The law also called for blacks to board buses at the rear door; when the white section of a bus had been filled, black passengers

Deputy sheriff D. H. Lackey fingerprints Rosa Parks in Montgomery, Alabama, in February 1956. The previous December, Parks's refusal to give up her bus seat to a white man had triggered a boycott that virtually paralyzed the Alabama capital.

A North Carolina girl uses a public fountain to quench her thirst in the 1950s. The "ultimate tragedy of segregation," noted the Reverend Martin Luther King, Jr., was that blacks "were so conditioned" to it "that they submissively adjusted themselves to things as they were."

were required to give up their seats to newly boarding whites. Even if a bus carried few whites, blacks were not permitted to use the front seats. Thus, after a long day of work, black men and women might find themselves standing next to an empty seat for the entire trip home, even though no white person ever claimed the seat.

Over the years this arrangement had been more or less accepted by Montgomery's black residents, although not without resentment. Many blacks feared reprisals from their white employers if they made any trouble. Others were so conditioned to segregation that it simply did not occur to them to fight it, preferring instead to adjust to things as they were.

At various times, however, some Montgomery residents had resisted. In early 1955, for example, 15-year-old Claudette Colvin had refused to give up her bus seat to a white passenger. Called to the scene by the bus driver, police officers had handcuffed the teenager, forcibly removed her from the bus, then arrested her. Concerned, a group of black citizens quickly took up the matter with the bus line's chief and the police commissioner.

After hearing the citizens' complaint of improper treatment, transportation officials promised that things would change, and Police Commissioner Dave Birmingham said the city would issue a clear statement about bus-seating regulations. In fact, nothing changed, and no statement appeared.

Though the Colvin case led to no improvement in

Bus riders in Dallas, Texas, seat themselves in the South's traditional pattern: whites to the front, blacks to the rear. Black southerners, leaders and common people alike, had long detested this practice, but it took a middle-aged department-store seamstress— Rosa Parks—to defy it openly.

conditions on the city bus lines, it did provide Montgomery's black community with an outlet for their long-pent-up feelings of resentment and frustration. Everyone seemed to have experienced, or known someone who had experienced, the kind of treatment undergone by Claudette Colvin, either on the buses or in some other realm of life in the segregated city.

The case of Emmett Till was also on the mind of Montgomery residents. In the summer of 1955, Till, a black 14-year-old from Chicago, had gone to the tiny Mississippi town of Money to visit relatives. While staying with his great-uncle Mose Wright, Emmett had accompanied some local boys to Bryant's Market, a nearby white-owned grocery store. The details of what happened are still somewhat murky, but Emmett appears to have boasted to the local boys that he had a white girlfriend back in Chicago.

Emmett's friends then challenged him to go into the store and talk with the white proprietor, Carolyn Bryant. Emmett took the challenge, went in, bought some candy, and left. On his way out of the store, he turned to Bryant and said, "Bye, baby." In the racist atmosphere of rural Mississippi, such words, spoken by a black male of any age to a white female of any age, were not taken lightly. When Bryant's husband, Roy, a trucker, returned home and heard about the black boy's visit to the store, he went into action immediately, enlisting his half-brother, J. W. Milam, to drive him out to Mose Wright's home.

Arriving just before dawn, Bryant and Milam demanded that Wright produce Emmett. Terrified, the 64-year-old farmer awakened the boy and brought him to the men, who hustled him into Milam's pickup truck. Three days later, Emmett's body was found in the Tallahatchie River. It was almost unrecognizable; the boy had been savagely beaten and mutilated, one side of his head had been bashed in, one eye was missing, and one bullet was lodged in his skull.

Weighting the body down was a heavy cotton-gin fan, attached to the neck by a length of barbed wire. Long afterward, J. W. Milam smiled as he recalled his last words to Emmett: "Boy, you ain't never going to see the sun come up again."

When Emmett's distraught mother, Mamie Till Mobley, learned that the state of Mississippi planned to bury her son's body immediately, she protested so sharply that reluctant officials permitted her to have the body shipped to Chicago. Mastering her grief and horror, Mobley ordered an open-casket funeral. "I wanted the whole world to see what I had seen," the 33-year-old schoolteacher said later. "There was no way I could describe what was in that box. No way. And I just wanted the world to see." The resulting publicity forced Mississippi to try the prime murder suspects.

After hearing extensive testimony—from Mose Wright, who, with incredible courage for a black man in 1955 Mississippi, pointed to the killers in court; from neighbors who saw the men driving Emmett in their truck; from people who heard a boy screaming in Milam's barn the night of Emmett's abduction— the all-white jury listened to the men's lawyer. "I am sure," said attorney John Whitten, "that every Anglo-Saxon one of you has the courage to acquit these men." He was not disappointed. The jury took just under an hour to clear Bryant and Milam of all charges.

Alabama's racial climate was not dissimilar to that of its Mississippi neighbor. A few years before the Till tragedy, a 16-year-old black Alabamian, Jeremiah Reeves, had confessed, under heavy police pressure, to raping a white woman. He had later retracted his confession, convincing most legal observers of his innocence, but after seven years of appeals, Alabama executed him. For the blacks of Montgomery and other southern communities, Reeves's fate was both

Emmett Till, a clear-eyed and friendly 14-year-old from Chicago, smiles before leaving to visit his Mississippi relatives in 1955. Within days, the teenager would be at the bottom of the Tallahatchie River, viciously murdered for the crime of saying "Bye, baby" to a white woman.

frightening and hard to accept; they knew, all too well, that white men accused of raping black women were rarely even arrested, and that if they were, they were almost invariably released.

Into this environment stepped a young clergyman named Martin Luther King, Jr. A native southerner, the young Boston University graduate had been offered a job as pastor of Montgomery's Dexter Avenue Baptist Church. King and his wife, Coretta, had deliberated long over the offer, for it meant returning to the South, the center of racial discrimination. In the end, however, they recognized in the call an opportunity to give their service where it was most needed. King later wrote in his memoir *Stride Toward Freedom*,

> Since racial discrimination was most intense in the South, we felt that some of the Negroes who had received a portion of their training in other sections of the country should return to share their broader contacts and educational experience in its solution. Moreover, despite having to sacrifice much of the cultural life we loved, despite the existence of Jim Crow, which kept reminding us at all times of the color of our skin, we had the feeling that something remarkable was unfolding in the South, and we wanted to be on hand to witness it.

King split his time during the first few months in Montgomery between attending to the business of the church and completing his doctoral thesis. He would write for three hours each morning and evening, spending his days getting to know the members of the church, preparing his Sunday sermon, and familiarizing himself with the social and political climate of Montgomery.

One thing he quickly learned was that the city's social service organizations that tended to the needs of the black community were disorganized and fragmented. Although there were many committed leaders, they rarely came together for united action. He noted later that he found Montgomery's black profes-

The Reverend Martin Luther King, Jr., was 25 years old when he and his wife, Coretta, moved to Montgomery, Alabama, in 1954. Within a few months, the young clergyman would find himself the leader of one of the strongest rights movements in American history.

sionals apathetic, and the black ministers, with a few notable exceptions, "aloof from the area of social responsibility." How were they to confront the crippling effects of segregation, King wondered, if they did not root their sermons in the present, if they did not draw out of the Bible the responsibility of Christians to confront social inequality?

One group, however, had been actively engaged in seeking to change the laws governing segregation on buses: the Women's Political Council (WPC), headed by Jo Ann Gibson Robinson. The WPC had been founded in 1946 by Dr. Mary Fair Burks, chair of the English department at Alabama State University, to fight for equal opportunity under the law.

Because of its proximity to the college, the group was composed chiefly of professional women, including educators, social workers, and community workers.

Six years before King's arrival in Montgomery, Robinson herself had been forced to give up her bus seat to a white passenger, even though there were only two other persons on the bus. The indignity of this experience weighed heavily on Robinson. Realizing that little had changed since the incident, she began to consider a black boycott of city buses as a solution. Robinson brought her suggestion to the attention of the WPC, even though, as she recalled in a memoir, she did "not have the slightest idea how—without involving others who might get hurt—to begin a boycott against the bus company that would put that company out of business." The WPC, she added, "took the idea under advisement."

Along with Robinson, King conferred with E. D. Nixon, another Montgomery leader who understood the importance of social activism. Nixon, a member of the Brotherhood of Sleeping Car Porters, a former NAACP official, and the head of the local Progressive Democrats, was deeply respected by Montgomery's black community. For some time he had been eager to find a test case to clarify the issue of segregation on public buses. What he wanted was the arrest of an individual whose character was so far above reproach that the city's civil rights activists would be able to appeal the segregation law all the way to the Supreme Court, where it might be overturned, as had happened in *Brown v. Board of Education*.

In recent months three black people had been arrested for challenging Montgomery's bus-segregation law. In each instance, however, Nixon had discovered something in the arrestee's background that could be exploited by a good prosecutor. Such was Nixon's weight in Montgomery that these cases were not appealed. If only someone were arrested, thought

Nixon, who carried such moral authority and strength of character that no prosecutor would be able to deflect attention from the injustice of the segregation laws. Then, on Thursday, December 1, 1955, Nixon's wish was granted.

That evening, Rosa L. Parks left her job in the tailor shop of the Montgomery Fair department store and, as she did every day, climbed aboard the Cleveland Avenue bus. On this occasion, the only vacant seat was situated just behind the "white" section. Although there were other black riders standing on the bus, none had taken the seat, so Parks made her way down the aisle and seated herself next to a black man. Two black women sat across the aisle from them.

After three stops, a white man boarded the bus, and the driver asked Parks and the others in her row to clear it for the new passenger. They refused. "You'd better make it light on yourselves and let me have those seats," responded the driver. The newly boarded white man made no indication that he wanted the blacks to move, but the three others on Parks's row got to their feet. Parks remained seated. The driver grew impatient. "If you don't stand up," he told Parks, "I'm going to have you arrested." She told him to go ahead and do that.

She did not know it yet, but in one stubborn moment of disobedience, Parks had started a movement that would change Montgomery and the rest of the South forever. As she later recalled,

I had had problems with bus drivers over the years, because I didn't see fit to pay my money into the front and then go around to the back. Sometimes bus drivers wouldn't permit me to get on the bus, and I had been evicted from the bus. . . . One of the things that made this get so much publicity was the fact that the police were called in and I was placed under arrest. See, if I had just been evicted from the bus and he hadn't placed me under arrest or had any charges brought against me, it probably could have been just another incident.

Here was the moment E. D. Nixon had been waiting for. He went to the police station, posted Parks's bond, then discussed the day's events with members of the Women's Political Council. The next morning he called the Reverend Martin Luther King, Jr., and told him that a decision had been made to press for a complete boycott of Montgomery's buses. "Only through a boycott," Nixon told King excitedly, "can we make it clear to the white folks that we will not accept this type of treatment any longer." With the help of the Reverend Ralph Abernathy, Nixon

Local activist E. D. Nixon accompanies Rosa Parks as she enters Montgomery's courthouse to be arraigned for violating the city's segregation laws. Found guilty, Parks immediately appealed, thus establishing a major test case to clarify the segregation issue.

and King began calling all the city's black ministers to spread word of the proposal.

On Friday evening, Montgomery's black civic and religious leaders crowded into King's Dexter Avenue church. By then news of Parks's arrest had spread throughout the city. After the idea of the boycott was floated among the gathered leaders, a brief period of confusion followed during which a flurry of questions arose from the floor: How long would the boycott last? How would it be organized? How would the black citizens of Montgomery get to their jobs? But even without all the answers, the leaders unanimously agreed to go ahead with the boycott.

Those at the meeting finally decided to call a one-day boycott on the following Monday, December 5. They also decided to hold a citywide black meeting on Monday evening, at a church led by the Reverend A. W. Wilson. That left the organizers with only the weekend to spread the word of these two momentous steps. A small group of people, including King and Robinson, prepared leaflets to be distributed throughout the black community. In the early hours of Sunday morning, they completed the final text, which read:

> Don't ride the bus to work, to town, to school, or any place Monday, December 5.
> Another Negro woman has been arrested and put in jail because she refused to give up her bus seat.
> Don't ride the buses to work, to town, to school, or anywhere on Monday. If you work, take a cab, or share a ride or walk.
> Come to a mass meeting, Monday at 7:00 P.M., at the Holt Street Baptist Church for further instruction.

The leaflets were distributed, and there was little the boycott leaders could do but wait to see what would happen Monday morning. King and his wife decided between themselves that if at least 60 percent of Montgomery blacks stayed off the buses, the boycott could be considered successful. Then the protest got a boost from an unexpected quarter. Somehow, news of the boycott had been picked up by the *Montgomery Advertiser*, and the newspaper's story about the upcoming action helped spread the word to anyone who had not yet seen a leaflet.

Late Sunday night King learned that the city's black taxi companies had agreed to assist the boycotters by transporting them for the same price as a bus ride. King went to sleep anxious but excited; dawn might bring a truly new day in Montgomery. On Monday morning he got up at 5:30, poured himself a cup of coffee, then heard his wife calling to him. The first bus of the day was passing by the Kings' home.

King walked to the window. To his and his wife's delighted surprise, the bus carried only one person, the driver. Fifteen minutes later, another bus passed by. It, too, was empty. The next bus carried two riders, both white. Elated, King jumped into his car and set out to see what was happening in other neighborhoods. Wherever he looked, the buses were empty. During the rest of the morning rush hour, King spotted only eight black riders. With an unhoped-for compliance of almost 100 percent, the boycott was a success.

Around the city, blacks watched the buses roll by, cheering when they saw no passengers. In some cases, the buses were followed by police cars; city officials had spread the false news that black "goon squads" were harassing blacks who rode the buses. King recalled that one student who had helped an older woman cross a street had been charged with "intimidating passengers." In fact, no one had been bothered for riding the bus. As King put it, "the only harassment anyone faced was that of his own conscience."

Later that morning, Rosa Parks was found guilty of violating the city's segregation laws and fined $10 plus court costs. The case was immediately appealed, establishing it as the test case that the Montgomery leaders had awaited so long. After the success of the boycott, the leaders knew they had started something big.

Yet questions remained: Was the boycott sustainable? How could the energy and the yearning for justice embodied by the black citizens' boycott be channeled into an effective movement? How could the black leaders contain the understandable rage that had now bubbled to the surface, and how could they direct it toward a practical purpose? Before any movement could take shape, these questions would have to be answered. Fortunately for the people of Montgomery, they had among themselves some of the finest moral voices and strategic minds in the nation.

A rolling symbol of victory for blacks, a Montgomery bus plies its route carrying no one but a driver. The vehicle, normally crowded with African Americans on their way to work, remained empty because of the citywide boycott called by the city's black civic and religious leaders.

7

WALKING TO VICTORY

On the afternoon of December 5, 1955, Martin Luther King, Jr., met with other Montgomery leaders to plan that night's citywide black meeting. Agreeing that the Montgomery protest needed organization, the leaders formed the Montgomery Improvement Association (MIA) and unanimously elected King as president.

King's first assignment was to address the gathering that night, but by the time he got home he had only a half hour to collect his thoughts. He had decided that he had a dual responsibility that evening: he would have to lay out a clear rationale for continuing the boycott, a rationale grounded in the fundamental injustice of segregation. At the same time, he would have to convince the assembled masses that they must not be moved to violence, that they must win the white establishment over by the moral force of their position. Oddly, the great orator found himself gripped by fear, so great was the challenge of reconciling these two demands. As the moments

The Reverend Martin Luther King, Jr., makes a characteristically eloquent gesture from his pulpit. Although the Montgomery bus boycott depended on many dedicated people, it was King's fervor and charisma that kept the protest on track.

passed, King realized that he would not be able to arrange his thoughts on paper before the beginning of the meeting, and would have to deliver his speech impromptu.

As he approached the Holt Street Church, King was surprised and deeply moved to discover that the turnout was tremendous. From the size of the crowd, it was clear that not everyone would be able to get into the church. After making his way inside, King found his way up to the pulpit. Television crews had already assembled around the packed room. After the singing of "Onward, Christian Soldiers" and subsequent prayers, King was introduced. With no notes to draw from, he began to speak.

> He talked about the humiliation of the daily oppression experienced by the black citizens of Montgomery. "There comes a time," he said, "that people get tired," and have no recourse other than protest. He spoke of the patience that the black community had shown over many years of unfair treatment. But, he added, the time had come when patience had worn thin. He spoke of the tactics employed by the White Citizens' Council and the Ku Klux Klan. "Their methods lead to violence and lawlessness," he said. "But in our protest there will be no cross burnings. No white person will be taken from his home by a hooded Negro mob and brutally murdered. There will be no threats and intimidation. We will be guided by the highest principles of law and order."

By the end of the evening, the meeting had approved the continuation of the boycott for as long as the buses of Montgomery remained segregated. A list of three demands was drawn up, to be presented to the Montgomery city commissioners. As King wrote in *Stride Toward Freedom*, the black citizens of the city would not return to the buses until: courteous treatment by the bus operators was guaranteed; passengers were seated on a first-come, first-served basis, "Negroes seating from the back of the bus toward the front while whites seated from the front toward the back"; and black bus operators were employed on predominantly black routes.

Of course the Montgomery officials were not about to give in without a fight. Even beyond their own biases, reinforced by the cultural values of white southern society, these officials simply could not believe that the black community would have the organization and discipline to keep the boycott going. In fact, at first some blacks shared that thought. If the boycott fizzled out quickly, it would show a lack of cohesion in the black community. A one-day show of force, on the other hand, could be used as a bargaining chip for incremental gains.

As it was, the boycott proceeded smoothly and methodically. For many of Montgomery's black residents, the long daily walks to and from work became a source of pride, a burden that took on new meaning in the context of protest. One elderly woman, asked if she was worn out by the arduous trek she was now required to make, responded with simple eloquence: "My feets is tired, but my soul is at rest."

For those unwilling or unable to walk, transportation became a more complicated matter. At the start of the boycott, black taxi drivers had agreed to shuttle blacks to work and school, but Police Commissioner Clyde Sellers had soon informed King that according

Montgomery workers emerge from a church-owned "boycott bus" in May 1956. At this stage of the strike, the city's African Americans had transportation well under control—much to the chagrin of the white community.

to city law, all taxis had to charge a minimum fare. It became clear that the boycotters would have to arrange some kind of car pool. More than 150 people immediately volunteered their cars for such a service. Working hastily, the MIA devised a system of 48 dispatch stations and 42 pickup stations. With the aid of black postal workers who knew the city inside and out, the MIA planners divided Montgomery into sections based on the number of black workers who would need the car pool. Within a few days, King recalled,

> this system was working astonishingly well. The white opposition was so impressed at this miracle of quick organization that they had to admit in a White Citizens' Council meeting that the pool moved with "military precision." The MIA had worked out in a few nights a transportation problem that the bus company had grappled with for many years.

When city officials finally understood the depth of the protesters' commitment, they took action. Mayor W. A. Gayle and Police Chief Sellers called on the head of the Montgomery City Lines, J. H. Bagley, to join them in a meeting with the boycott leaders. After hours of discussion, Bagley flatly asserted that any accommodation of the MIA's three basic demands would represent a breach of city segregation laws. "And as far as bus drivers are concerned," he said, referring to the MIA's request for black drivers, "we have no intention now or in the foreseeable future of hiring Negroes."

King left the meeting sure of at least one thing: there would be no change in the bus-segregation rules until the city's basic segregation laws themselves were overturned.

As the appeal in the Rosa Parks case made its way slowly through the judicial process, the MIA and King met further setbacks. King's enemies—the conservative leaders of Montgomery's white population—began to circulate ugly rumors about King: he was not a worthy leader, they said; he was a man concerned only about making a name for himself. He sought to profit financially from the protest and had already bought himself a new car with money raised from gullible blacks. King did his best to ignore such lies, but after days of this kind of talk, he began to grow edgy. Hoping to remove himself as a distraction to the campaign, he offered his resignation at the next MIA executive committee meeting. Instantly and vehemently, King's peers rejected his offer.

On a Saturday in late January 1956, Montgomery civic officials made a surprise announcement: a group of prominent black clergymen had reached an agreement with the city, and they were calling off the boycott. King responded to this dangerous hoax speedily. Calling the local ministers to an emergency meeting, he asked them to tell their congregations that the rumor was false: the boycott was by no means over. He sent aides around town to spread the same news. Disaster was averted, but at a price.

An overflow crowd at St. John's African Methodist Episcopal Church patiently awaits news from within. Held some three months after the Montgomery boycott's onset, the St. John's meeting drew 4,000 citizens, the vast majority of whom voted to continue the strike.

The city's white establishment met King's moves with what he called its new "get tough" policy. Policemen began pulling over car-pool drivers, inspecting their licenses for any outstanding violations. The police harassed boycotters waiting for their rides by informing them that they could be arrested for hitchhiking. Shortly thereafter, patrolmen arrested King himself, charging him with exceeding the speed limit by five miles per hour. Taken to the city jail and fingerprinted, King was released after the Reverend Ralph Abernathy posted his bond. On his return home, the fighting clergyman discovered a small army of well-wishers and found that his determination to see the boycott through was stronger than ever.

King would need that strength in the days to come. He had been receiving threatening letters and phone calls since the beginning of the campaign, but by the middle of January, they were pouring in at the rate of 40 per day. On January 30, King was addressing an MIA meeting at Abernathy's First Baptist Church. At home, his wife was taking care of their two-month-old daughter and chatting with a friend in the living room when she heard an odd thump on the front porch. Trained to be calm in a crisis, Coretta Scott King was leading her friend to the back of the house just as they felt a tremendous force shake the whole house. Hurled to the porch seconds before, a bomb had filled the living room with broken glass and evil-smelling smoke.

Eight "criminals"—actually, black Montgomery's civic and religious leaders—line up after their February 1956 indictment for conspiring to encourage the bus boycott. Among the arrested activists are the Reverend Ralph D. Abernathy (far left); Citizens' Council manager Rufus Lewis (third from left); and the Reverend Leroy R. Bennett, Interdenominational Council president (fourth from left).

As soon as he got the news, King rushed to his house, where he found hundreds of people already gathered. After checking on the welfare of his wife and daughter, King turned to the angry crowd, whose members were loudly cursing the perpetrators of this horrible act. Many people carried weapons. The mayor and police commissioner, who were also there, feared that violence might erupt. King wasted no time in addressing the crowd.

He encouraged them to return to their homes and put their weapons away. Looking out at the men and women on his lawn, he said,

> He who lives by the sword will perish by the sword. We must love our white brothers no matter what they do to us. We must make them know that we love them. Jesus still cries out in words that echo across the centuries: "Love your enemies; bless them that curse you; pray for them that despitefully use you." This is what we must live by. We must meet hate with love.

It soon became clear that intimidation tactics could not force the black community back onto the buses.

The city's white establishment decided that stronger measures would have to be taken. Sometime earlier, they had discovered an old state law that made it a conspiracy for two or more persons to obstruct the operation of a lawful business. Accordingly, on February 13, a Montgomery County grand jury (composed of 17 whites and one black) began targeting people who had been participating in the boycott. More than 100 people were indicted, including King. The indictment came while King was out of town. Before returning to Montgomery, he stopped in Atlanta to visit his parents.

King's father, the Reverend Martin Luther King, Sr., had been in a state of deep anxiety about his son's safety ever since the boycott

began. Now, he pleaded with his son not to return to Alabama. To bolster his argument, he gathered other respected black Atlanta leaders. The younger King listened patiently, then politely told the leaders that he had no choice but to go back. "My friends and associates are being arrested," he said. "It would be the height of cowardice for me to stay away. I would rather be in jail 10 years than desert my people now. I have begun the struggle, and I can't turn back. I have reached the point of no return."

King's powerful words won the leaders over to his position. A call was put through to the great NAACP lawyer (and future Supreme Court justice) Thurgood Marshall, who promised that King would have the best legal counsel available. King's father, far from admonishing his son, made an equally courageous decision to accompany him back to Montgomery.

King's trial began on March 19. The prosecution laid out its case that King had violated the state's antiobstruction law. King's impressive defense team, in turn, called 28 witnesses to document the injustice of segregation on the city's buses. One of them, Stella Brooks, said that one day, her husband had been asked to board from the back of the bus after paying his fare at the front. The back of the bus was so crowded that Brooks told the driver he would prefer to walk and asked for his dime back. Balking at this request, the driver called a policeman, who ordered Brooks off the bus. He refused to go without his refund. Without warning the policeman shot him, and he later died.

Another witness, Martha Walker, told the court that she had once been helping her blind husband off a bus. As Mr. Walker followed his wife, the driver closed the door, catching Walker's leg, then moved

Addressing reporters at the Montgomery County Courthouse in March 1956, King (seen with his wife, Coretta) discusses his upcoming boycott trial. Following his conviction, he said, "We will continue to protest in the same spirit of nonviolence and passive resistance, using the weapon of love."

the bus forward. Martha Walker called out to the driver to stop, but he kept his foot on the gas, dragging the blind man down the street for some distance before he was able to break free.

Georgia Clinton told of the day she had paid her fare, then stepped off the bus to board from the back. Before she could climb aboard, it began to move, stranding her even though she had paid her fare. But "when they count the money," said Clinton, "they do not know Negro money from white money." Despite the power of these testimonials, the judge found King guilty of violating the law and fined him $500 plus court costs. "[Although] I was a convicted criminal,"

King said later, "I was proud of my crime. It was the crime of joining my people in a nonviolent protest against injustice."

In May 1956 the MIA filed a lawsuit in U.S. federal district court, attacking the city's segregation laws as a violation of the Constitution's Fourteenth Amendment. This argument had been used successfully in the 1954 school desegregation case, and King and his allies felt that it could be extended to other areas of segregation. With the case being heard in a federal court, the MIA's hopes were high. Here, protected from the sanctioned prejudice of the southern courts, they felt confident justice would prevail. They were right. Just under a month after it heard the case,

Coretta Scott King embraces her husband after he is found guilty of leading an illegal boycott. By now sure that their protest would end in a defeat of Montgomery's segregation laws, supporters let out a rousing cheer.

Rosa Parks arrives at Montgomery's courthouse to be arraigned for taking part in the boycott. An obscure seamstress only a few months earlier, Parks had become—and would remain—one of the civil rights movement's most revered figures.

the court rendered its verdict. Two of the three members of the federal panel determined that segregation of city buses in Montgomery was unconstitutional. But the city appealed the decision, ensuring that the boycott would continue for many more months.

Montgomery's black residents held firm in their commitment to the boycott throughout the summer of 1956. As Rosa Parks's case made its way toward the Supreme Court, the city of Montgomery made a last-ditch effort to derail the boycott. In late October, the city of Montgomery went back to court, trying to get an injunction on car pools as a "public nuisance." If the city succeeded in this move, the boycott would be over. On November 13, King was sitting in court with the MIA's attorney, waiting for the judge to decide whether or not to ban the car pools. At noon, during a recess in the hearing, a commotion broke the calm of the courtroom. Observing reporters in a flurry of activity, King wondered what was up. His concern was quickly resolved when an Associated Press newsman handed him a wire service bulletin.

> **King could scarcely believe what he was reading: it was the one event he and his allies had been waiting for. The bulletin said, "The United States Supreme Court today affirmed a decision of a special three-judge U.S. district court in declaring Alabama's state and local laws requiring segregation on buses unconstitutional." The Court had not even bothered to hear any arguments in the case in making its decision.**

The Montgomery bus boycott would continue until the Court's official order reached the city. In the meantime, the Ku Klux Klan organized a large rally. Normally, the city's black residents would have stayed indoors, fearful of what might happen to them if they appeared while the hooded men stormed through town. This time, however, the MIA encouraged blacks to come outside and watch the Klan march as though it were a parade. As 40 carloads of Klansmen drove by, blacks looked on from their porches. Some even waved. Realizing that their effort at intimidation had failed, the Klansmen gave up after only a few blocks.

Finally, on December 20, the integration order arrived. The MIA urged black riders to be direct in claiming their newly won right to sit where they pleased, but not to gloat or be in any way discourteous to white riders. On the morning of December 21, King boarded a city bus for the first time in more than a year. As he paid his fare, the driver greeted him with a smile. "I believe you are Reverend King, aren't you?" asked the driver. King replied that he was. "We are glad to have you this morning," the driver continued. King walked down the aisle and took a seat in one of the front rows. Next to him sat a white man. The ride—and indeed, the whole first day of integration—proceeded without incident.

Over the next few months, there were scattered incidents of violence as recalcitrant whites tried to block the progress made by Montgomery's blacks. These incidents were not wholly unexpected. The fear and prejudice of two centuries would not be changed overnight. But the citizens of Montgomery had made a bold beginning. As King had said when he called off the boycott,

> For more than 12 months now, we, the Negro citizens of Montgomery, have been engaged in a nonviolent protest against injustices and indignities experienced on city buses. We came to see that, in the long run, it is more honorable to walk in dignity than ride in humiliation.

It was a powerful message, one that would inspire countless others to champion the cause of racial justice in the years to come.

FURTHER READING

Aldred, Lisa. *Thurgood Marshall*. New York: Chelsea House, 1990.

Baldwin, James. *Go Tell It on the Mountain*. New York: Doubleday, 1981.

Bennett, Lerone, Jr. *Before the Mayflower*. New York: Penguin, 1985.

Brooks, Thomas R. *Walls Come Tumbling Down: A History of the Civil Rights Movement, 1940–1970*. Englewood Cliffs, NJ: Prentice-Hall, 1974.

Garrow, David J., ed. *The Montgomery Bus Boycott and the Women Who Started It*. Knoxville: University of Tennessee Press, 1987.

Jones, Leroi. *Blues People*. New York: Morrow, 1963.

King, Martin Luther, Jr. *Stride Toward Freedom: The Montgomery Story*. San Francisco: HarperCollins, 1986.

Kluger, Richard. *Simple Justice*. New York: Knopf, 1976.

Kugelmass, J. Alvin. *Ralph J. Bunche, Fighter for Peace*. New York: Messner, 1972.

Pfeffer, Paula F. *A. Philip Randolph, Pioneer of the Civil Rights Movement*. Baton Rouge: Louisiana State University Press, 1990.

Scott, Richard. *Jackie Robinson*. New York: Chelsea House, 1987.

Woodward, C. Vann. *The Strange Career of Jim Crow*. New York: Oxford University Press, 1966.

INDEX

PICTURE CREDITS

MARGARET DORNFELD is a book editor specializing in history and literary criticism. She lives in Brooklyn, where she sings gospel with the Lafayette Avenue Inspirational Ensemble.

DARLENE CLARK HINE, senior consulting editor of the MILESTONES IN BLACK AMERICAN HISTORY series, is the John A. Hannah Professor of American History at Michigan State University. She is the author of numerous books and articles on black women's history, as well as the editor of the two-volume *Black Women in America: An Historical Encyclopedia* (1993). Her most recent work is *Hine Sight: Black Women and the Re-Construction of American History*.

CLAYBORNE CARSON, senior consulting editor of the MILESTONES IN BLACK AMERICAN HISTORY series, is a professor of history at Stanford University. His first book, *In Struggle: SNCC and the Black Awakening of the 1960s* (1981), won the Frederick Jackson Turner Prize of the Organization of American Historians. He is the director of the Martin Luther King, Jr., Papers Project, which will publish 12 volumes of King's writings.